Eidotheosophy
Divine Wisdom and
Biblical Mythology

Vanida Plamondon

EIDOTHEOSOPHY - DIVINE WISDOM AND BIBLICAL MYTHOLOGY

First edition. December 1, 2024.

Copyright © 2024 Vanida Plamondon.

ISBN: 979-8230169918

Written by Vanida Plamondon.

Eidotheosophy

Eidotheosophy is a term I created to describe a way of thinking that helps us make sense of biblical mythology in a more grounded, reasoned way. The word itself comes from two parts: "Eido," which refers to knowledge or insight, and "theosophy," which traditionally refers to knowledge about god or divine wisdom. So, at its core, eidotheosophy is about seeking divine wisdom while separating it from the human influences that have crept into our understanding of the lessons from biblical mythology. It's a way of looking at biblical mythology, not as a religious document but as a complex set of ideas that have been shaped by both divine insight and human interests.

The central thesis of eidotheosophy is simple but profound: there is a distinct difference between divine wisdom and the way humanity has interpreted or altered that wisdom to suit personal, political, or cultural interests. I believe that much of the conflict and confusion we see in theological discussions comes from not distinguishing between these two influences. Human beings have, throughout history, inserted their own ideas and biases into the interpretation of biblical mythology. These additions often have more to do with human desires for power, control, or validation than with a truly divine message.

Eidotheosophy encourages us to look at biblical mythology and examine it with a critical, reasoned approach. We need to ask ourselves which parts of the narrative reflect true divine wisdom and which parts reflect the influence of human interests. This isn't about rejecting biblical mythology but about recognizing the layers of human influence that have been added over time. The goal is to separate divine wisdom from the ideologies that were inserted by people who had their own agendas. This way of thinking invites us to use reason, logic, and historical analysis as tools to help us identify the parts of the mythology that still hold true to divine wisdom and those that might need to be reconsidered or discarded.

The reason this is so important is that when we confuse human-driven ideology with divine wisdom, we end up with a warped view of both faith and its role in society. Theological beliefs and ideas from biblical mythology can get lost in the noise of human politics, power struggles, and personal beliefs. Eidotheosophy is a way of sifting through that noise, focusing on the parts of the mythology that have enduring value, and separating them from the parts that no longer serve us or may even be harmful. It's about creating a space where we can have a more honest, clear, and open conversation about what is truly divine and what is merely a product of human history.

Divine Wisdom Vs. Human Distortion

The idea of separating divine wisdom from human distortions is rooted in the simple, yet powerful, belief that divine wisdom is pure and untainted, while human interpretations of such wisdom are often influenced by personal biases, cultural norms, and historical circumstances. To really understand why this distinction is so important, we have to first recognize that biblical mythology was shaped by the people who passed it down. These individuals weren't just passive recipients of divine wisdom. They were living in specific times and places, and their interpretations of such wisdom were coloured by the societies they lived in, the politics they were part of, and the personal ambitions they held. So, when we consider such mythology, we have to ask ourselves: what part of this reflects divine wisdom and what part reflects human interests?

This idea isn't just about skepticism or rejecting tradition. It's about understanding that humans, by nature, are prone to self-interest. When we look at the way biblical mythology has been interpreted over the centuries, it's easy to see how certain parts have been used to justify human desires for power, control, and influence. For example, the way certain biblical passages have been used to support systems of inequality, like slavery or patriarchy, doesn't necessarily reflect divine wisdom. It reflects how people have misused those teachings for their own gain. When we take a step back, we can see that these human distortions are not divine wisdom but are the result of people trying to shape the teachings to fit their own worldviews.

So, the foundation for separating divine wisdom from human distortion is based on the idea that divine wisdom is constant and eternal, while human interpretations are always subject to change, influenced by the contexts in which they are made. This means that when we approach biblical mythology, we can't take everything at face value. We need to recognize the historical and cultural context in which certain ideas were introduced and ask whether those ideas still serve us today or whether they are just remnants of a past that no longer holds relevance. This doesn't mean that we throw out this mythology altogether. Instead, it means that we approach it with a discerning eye, recognizing which parts are truly divine and which are merely human constructions.

This process requires a willingness to be critical, not just of the mythology itself, but of the way it has been interpreted and used over time. It's about understanding that just because something has been traditionally accepted doesn't mean it's free from human influence. The challenge, then, is to sift through the layers of human distortion and get to the heart of what is truly divine. This requires a mindset that is open to rethinking old interpretations and willing to discard those ideas that no longer align with what we understand to be good, just, and true. By doing so, we can begin to separate divine wisdom from the wisdom of man, creating a clearer path forward for how we live out our faith today.

Foundations Of Biblical Mythology

When we examine biblical mythology, it's important to remember that it isn't just a standalone document that appeared out of nowhere. biblical mythology is deeply rooted in the cultural and religious contexts of the people who wrote it. It draws heavily from the customs, traditions, and mythology of surrounding nations and cultures, especially the Canaanites. These influences shaped the stories, symbols, and ideas found in the biblical texts. The ancient Israelites didn't create their religious ideas in isolation. They were part of a larger world, one where various peoples and their gods interacted, fought, and shared ideas. This means that when we examine biblical mythology, we're not just reading something that exists in a vacuum; we're looking at a collection of stories that were shaped by a blend of different religious and cultural practices over time.

The Canaanites, for instance, had their own gods and myths that overlapped in many ways with the early Hebrew traditions. Many of the stories that make up the foundation of biblical mythology, such as creation narratives or flood myths, share striking similarities with those from other ancient cultures in the Near East. Take the story of the flood, for example. The biblical account of Noah's Ark bears a strong resemblance to earlier Mesopotamian stories like the Epic of Gilgamesh, where a great flood wipes out humanity. These shared elements suggest that biblical writers were not creating stories from scratch but were influenced by the broader cultural landscape of their time.

Understanding this historical and cultural context is crucial when we try to separate divine wisdom from human interests. It helps explain why certain themes and motifs appear in biblical mythology that are also present in other ancient mythologies. These similarities don't necessarily undermine the value of the biblical text, but they do remind us that this mythology is a product of its time. It's a reflection of the customs, beliefs, and ideas that the ancient Israelites shared with their neighbours. And just as the mythology of other cultures was influenced by their social and political circumstances, so too was this mythology shaped by the needs and desires of the people who wrote it.

So, when we approach biblical mythology, we need to keep in mind that these stories were not created in a vacuum. They were influenced by the religious traditions and mythologies of neighbouring peoples within the region. This doesn't mean this mythology lacked value or truth. It just means that we must recognize the layers of influence that shaped these stories and be mindful of how human interests and cultural exchanges played a role in the way divine wisdom was understood and recorded. By doing so, we can begin to distinguish between the enduring truths of divine wisdom and the human interpretations and adaptations that have shaped the text over time.

Eidotheosophy Need Not Be Limited To Biblical Mythology

The concept of eidotheosophy isn't something that has to be applied strictly to biblical mythology. While I've found it most meaningful in the context of the christian mythology, the principles of eidotheosophy can be applied to any spiritual or religious tradition. The core of eidotheosophy is rooted in the idea of "knowing" or experiencing the divine presence, often referred to as the "holy spirit," within ourselves. This guiding force influences our actions and thoughts, leading us toward greater understanding and wisdom. However, the discernment between divine wisdom and human distortion comes not from the holy spirit itself but from the tools of knowledge, reason, and understanding that we develop. These tools allow us to separate pure divine wisdom from the influences of human interests, which have often distorted or added layers to spiritual teachings.

In my personal experience, I have felt the holy spirit as an active presence within me, influencing my thoughts and actions. It's not a passive feeling but an ongoing influence that encourages me to seek deeper understanding and wisdom. While I believe this divine presence shapes and influences my perspective, it does not, on its own, grant me the ability to distinguish between what is truly divine and what is human interpretation or distortion. That distinction requires something more: the active application of knowledge, logic, and critical thinking. These are the tools we need to analyze the teachings we receive, whether they come from religious texts, personal experiences, conventional knowledge, or societal norms.

When I consider biblical mythology, I see it as a collection of stories that were shaped by human authors that were influenced by the holy spirit to some degree. This mythology reflects this divine influence, yet it was inevitably filtered through the human lens of the writers, their cultures, and their time. The task of eidotheosophy is to apply the tools of understanding to sift through these layers, to recognize the divine wisdom that the holy spirit may have inspired while also identifying the human interests, biases, and distortions that may have shaped how that wisdom was expressed.

In this framework, the holy spirit's role is to guide us spiritually, to influence our hearts and minds toward a deeper connection with the divine, but it's through reason, study, and reflection that we discern which teachings are rooted in divine wisdom and which may have been altered by human hands. The holy spirit may lead us toward the truth, but it's through the careful application of knowledge and understanding that we are able to identify that truth. This process is central to eidotheosophy, as it helps us navigate the complex relationship between the divine and the human, between pure wisdom and the distortions that have crept into religious traditions over time.

Interpreting Biblical Mythology

Since we cannot verify biblical mythology as entirely valid or reliable in terms of historical accuracy or divine origin, we have to approach it as a collection of Judaic and Christian myths. This means we must recognize that biblical mythology, like other mythologies, is a product of human culture, shaped by specific people, times, and places. That doesn't mean it's without value or wisdom, but it does mean that we do not have any reasonable cause to believe that it is infused with divine truth. We don't know how much divine wisdom, if any at all, is directly contained in biblical mythology. This is where eidotheosophy comes in, because it provides us with a framework to evaluate and sift through the different ideas presented in biblical mythology and discern which ones are most aligned with divine wisdom.

When we begin this examination of biblical mythology through the lens of eidotheosophy, the first step is to gather and consider everything that is said, every teaching or idea presented within the text. We don't make any immediate assumptions or dismiss anything outright. Instead, we approach it with an open mind, aware that the text could contain both human distortions and divine wisdom. Once we have a clear picture of what biblical mythology is presenting, the next step is to apply historical analysis and research. This means examining the context in which these ideas were written, considering the social, political, and cultural influences at play. This research helps us understand whether the teachings are truly reflective of divine wisdom or if they have been shaped by human interests or cultural norms.

The purpose of this examination is not to undermine biblical mythology but to give us the tools we need to separate the divine from the human. By doing this, we can begin to evaluate the ideas presented in the text based on their real-world impact and relevance. The key question we ask is whether these ideas benefit or improve the health of our minds, bodies, or communities. Does the ideology promote well-being, harmony, and justice? Does it support actions that lead to healthier, more just, and more compassionate societies? If the answer is yes, then we can reasonably argue that the ideology is aligned with divine wisdom. If the answer is no, then we must consider that this ideology may have been influenced more by human interests than by the divine.

This is how we determine which ideologies are truly divine according to the principles of eidotheosophy. It's not a simple matter of picking and choosing what feels right but requires a careful, methodical process of examining the teachings within biblical mythology and comparing them to the principles we know lead to healthier, more just, and more compassionate lives. By using historical analysis, research, and the tools of reason, we can begin to separate the enduring wisdom from the distortions and start to identify what is truly of divine origin.

Eidotheosophy Does Not Need Biblical Mythology

Eidotheosophy doesn't actually require biblical mythology to be a valid process. While I've been using biblical mythology as a framework for understanding how divine wisdom might be recognized and discerned, the core principles of eidotheosophy are much broader. It's a philosophy that stands on its own, regardless of religious background. The essence of eidotheosophy is the pursuit of genuine wisdom that benefits humanity, grounded in the idea that we can separate divine insights from human distortions. This philosophy is about seeking well-being, peace, compassion, and justice, values that transcend any one religious tradition. If we discard the trappings of "god's wisdom" as presented in any particular mythology, eidotheosophy remains a philosophy of universal human values, one that should be embraced and promoted for the good of society.

At its heart, eidotheosophy calls for a thoughtful and reasoned approach to life. It's about using the tools of knowledge, understanding, and reason to evaluate the world around us and our place in it. We don't need a specific mythological narrative to know that peace, justice, and compassion are worth striving for. These are values that can be recognized by anyone, regardless of their religious beliefs. The philosophy of eidotheosophy encourages people to think critically, to question assumptions, and to pursue ideas that promote the collective well-being of all. It's a philosophy that doesn't rely on the authority of ancient texts but instead calls on each of us to use our reason and understanding to shape a better world.

The reason eidotheosophy has been conceived in the context of the mythology known and understood by followers of the world's major religions is simple. Many of these religious traditions have long histories and have shaped the moral and ethical frameworks that guide billions of people. By introducing eidotheosophy to those who are already familiar with the mythologies of these religions, we can help bring them into the age of reason. This isn't about rejecting their faith or their beliefs but about offering a way to reconcile these teachings with the insights of reason and modern understanding. It's about showing that the values embedded in their traditions, values such as compassion, justice, and peace, are compatible with a reasoned, evidence-based approach to living a good life.

Eidotheosophy, in this way, becomes a bridge. It allows people to move beyond the confines of literal interpretations of sacred texts and toward a deeper understanding of the principles that those texts were meant to teach. It's about bringing believers into a space where they can see their faith not as something opposed to reason but as something that can coexist with it. By promoting well-being, peace, compassion, and justice, eidotheosophy aligns with the best aspects of the human experience and encourages us all to strive for a world where these values are prioritized. It's a philosophy that, at its core, is rooted in the idea that reason, compassion, and justice should guide us toward a better future for all.

Religion Is Shaped By Human Interests

Theological and religious discussions today have often been shaped more by human interests than by the divine wisdom they claim to represent. This happens for a number of reasons, but one of the biggest factors is the way that religious ideas have historically been used to support particular power structures or societal norms. Throughout history, those in positions of authority, whether they were kings, priests, or political leaders, have often manipulated religious teachings to justify their power, control the masses, and enforce societal rules that suited their interests. When we look at many of the theological debates that have taken place over the centuries, we can see that they often reflect these human interests more than any objective truth or divine insight.

One clear example of this is how religious institutions have historically positioned themselves as the sole arbiters of truth. Instead of encouraging believers to seek out knowledge and wisdom for themselves, many religious leaders have discouraged critical thinking and fostered a sense of dependency on religious authority. This was often done because religious authority gave those in charge immense power. Theological discussions were shaped to maintain this power dynamic, with certain ideas being emphasized while others were silenced. This allowed the leaders to control how people thought about the world and their place in it, often to the benefit of the leaders themselves.

Additionally, many of the religious ideas that have been passed down through generations reflect the cultural and societal norms of the times in which they were written. Biblical mythology, for example, was shaped by the values of the people who created it, many of whom lived in patriarchal societies where men had the most power and authority. This has influenced much of the theological discussion around gender roles, authority, and morality. Religious texts, instead of being purely divine wisdom, often reflect the biases and interests of the societies that produced them. This is why we see so much conflict and disagreement in theological discussions today. Different people and groups interpret these texts in ways that reflect their own interests, whether those are political, social, or personal.

It is also worth noting that religious ideas have often been weaponized in modern times, used to justify things like war, inequality, and discrimination. In many cases, religious ideas have been twisted to serve political or ideological agendas. Leaders have used religious language and symbols to rally people to their cause, sometimes even to the point of violence. This is a clear example of how human interests have shaped religious discussions. The divine wisdom that many believe is at the heart of religion becomes obscured when it is used to justify harm or oppression.

All of this leads to a situation where many religious discussions today are more about defending one's own interests or preserving power than about seeking truth or wisdom. The focus shifts from understanding the deeper meaning behind religious teachings to using those teachings to maintain the status quo or to serve a particular agenda. This is why, in my view, it is essential to recognize that much of what we see in theological discussions today is not necessarily divine wisdom but a reflection of human interests. Only by separating these two can we begin to approach a more honest and true understanding of what faith, and spirituality can offer.

The Gap Between Faith And Reason

The gap between faith and reason in contemporary society is one of the most significant challenges to how we approach questions of belief, morality, and truth. On one hand, faith often involves trust in something that transcends logic and evidence. It calls on people to embrace the unseen, to believe in concepts or beings that cannot be tested or verified by science. On the other hand, reason relies on observation, critical thinking, and evidence. It demands that we question what we are told, test our assumptions, and draw conclusions based on what can be demonstrated or proved. These two approaches to understanding the world sometimes feel like they exist on entirely different planes, and this perceived divide has caused tension and misunderstanding on both sides.

Part of the issue lies in how faith is presented within many religious traditions. Faith is often framed as unquestioning loyalty to a set of doctrines or teachings. This loyalty can create a resistance to inquiry, as believers may feel that questioning their faith risks undermining it. In some religious circles, doubt is treated as a moral failing or a sign of weakness, which discourages open dialogue and exploration. This approach fosters a kind of intellectual isolation where faith is shielded from the scrutiny that reason brings. When this happens, faith becomes rigid, unable to adapt or engage with new ideas, and it risks becoming disconnected from the realities of the world.

Reason, on the other hand, is sometimes presented in a way that dismisses or devalues faith altogether. There is a tendency among some proponents of reason to see faith as naive or irrelevant, something that belongs to the past rather than the present. This attitude can alienate people of faith and deepen the divide. It also overlooks the fact that faith, for many people, is not just about accepting doctrines but about finding meaning, purpose, and connection. Faith can be a powerful motivator for acts of kindness, justice, and love, values that reason also upholds. By dismissing faith entirely, reason misses the opportunity to engage with and understand the deeply human need for spiritual connection.

The gap between faith and reason is further complicated by cultural and societal factors. In some contexts, the two are pitted against each other as if they are in direct competition. Science and religion are often portrayed as being at odds, with no possibility of reconciliation. This narrative creates an unnecessary conflict where people feel they must choose one side or the other. It overlooks the potential for faith and reason to complement each other. Faith can provide the moral and emotional grounding that inspires inquiry and innovation, while reason can help clarify and refine the principles that guide our actions and beliefs.

Another factor contributing to the gap is the lack of tools or frameworks to bridge it. Many people do not know how to bring faith and reason into conversation with each other in a way that feels productive and respectful. There is a need for spaces where people can explore the intersections between these two ways of understanding the world. These spaces should encourage curiosity, openness, and a willingness to question without fear. They should also recognize that both faith and reason have limitations. Faith cannot answer every question, and reason cannot explain every mystery. By acknowledging these limitations, we create room for dialogue rather than division.

What makes this gap so tragic is that faith and reason, when brought together, have the potential to enrich and support each other. Faith, at its best, can inspire us to strive for justice, compassion, and hope. Reason, at its best, gives us the tools to understand the world and solve its problems. When we see them as partners rather than opponents, we can approach the complexities of life with both humility and confidence. We can hold onto our sense of wonder while also seeking clarity. Bridging the gap between faith and reason is not about diluting either one but about allowing them to inform and elevate each other in ways that serve humanity as a whole.

Divine Wisdom Shaping Moral, Ethical, And Theological Concepts

The role of the divine in shaping moral, ethical, and theological concepts in biblical mythology is a fascinating topic. When we read these stories, it is impossible to ignore the repeated assertion that god is the source of wisdom, guidance, and justice. Yet, as we examine these texts, we also see the fingerprints of the people who wrote them, their communities, and their historical contexts. The divine voice, as it appears in biblical mythology, often feels intertwined with the hopes, fears, and struggles of the cultures that produced these writings. This makes it both a source of inspiration and a reflection of human limitations.

The moral and ethical teachings in biblical mythology are often presented as coming directly from god. Stories like the Ten Commandments or the Sermon on the Mount are framed as divine revelations. These teachings emphasize values like justice, compassion, humility, and the importance of treating others well. They aim to guide people toward a better way of living, not only for the individual but also for the community. The divine, in these stories, is portrayed as a being who desires peace, fairness, and a harmonious society. These ideals resonate deeply because they reflect universal human concerns.

At the same time, biblical mythology contains a number of moral and ethical ideas that seem less about divine wisdom and more about the social realities of the time. Rules about slavery, gender roles, or the treatment of outsiders often reflect the norms and hierarchies of ancient societies. These teachings were likely influenced by the need to maintain order or protect the interests of those in power. It becomes harder to see the divine hand in these aspects of biblical mythology, as they seem more tied to human priorities than to a universal moral truth.

The theological concepts in biblical mythology also suggest a mix of divine inspiration and human interpretation. The portrayal of god varies widely, from a stern lawgiver to a loving parent to a warrior defending his people. These differing images of the divine likely arose from the diverse experiences and needs of the people who shaped these stories. In times of suffering or oppression, the idea of a god who delivers justice and rescues the downtrodden may have offered hope. In more stable times, the emphasis on a god of love and forgiveness might have helped maintain social harmony. These variations suggest that while people may have been inspired by a sense of the divine, their understanding of god was filtered through their own lives and circumstances.

This blending of divine influence and human context is what makes biblical mythology so compelling and challenging. On one hand, it offers glimpses of profound wisdom, calling people to live lives of integrity and purpose. On the other hand, it forces us to confront the ways in which human interests and biases can shape even our most sacred stories. By examining these texts carefully, we can begin to untangle the divine ideals from the human influences. This allows us to better appreciate the moral, ethical, and theological teachings that truly uplift and inspire, while also recognizing and setting aside the elements that reflect outdated or harmful ways of thinking.

Human Interests Shaping Moral, Ethical, And Theological Concepts

Human interests have always played a role in shaping religious texts and practices. It is hard to imagine how it could be otherwise. People are the ones who wrote down these stories, interpreted them, and decided how they should be used. They did this in the context of their own lives, communities, and cultures. These influences are woven into the fabric of religious texts and the practices that grew out of them.

One of the clearest ways human interests have shaped religious texts is through the inclusion of rules and laws that maintain social order. In ancient societies, religion was often a way to enforce a shared moral code. The laws in religious texts frequently address things like property rights, marriage, and punishment for crimes. While some of these laws reflect principles of fairness and justice, others seem more focused on preserving the power structures of the time. Rules about who could hold leadership positions or who had access to certain privileges often reinforced existing hierarchies. This kind of practical, human-centred thinking is hard to separate from the divine voice these texts claim to represent.

Religious practices have also been influenced by the need to create unity and identity within a community. Rituals and traditions help define who belongs and who does not. They give people a sense of shared purpose and connection. At the same time, they can also serve as tools for control. Leaders and institutions often use religious practices to maintain their authority and influence. The way certain rituals are framed as essential or non-negotiable can sometimes feel more like an assertion of power than a reflection of divine will.

Another way human interests shape religion is through the interpretation of texts. People have always tried to make sense of religious teachings in ways that align with their own beliefs, values, and goals. This is not necessarily a bad thing. It shows how adaptable and relevant these teachings can be. However, it also means that interpretations can be skewed to justify almost anything. Wars, oppression, and exclusion have all been defended using religious arguments. This does not mean the texts themselves call for these things, but it does show how flexible and open to manipulation they can be.

The process of canonization, where certain texts are chosen as sacred while others are left out, is another example. Decisions about which stories and teachings to include were made by people, often with specific agendas. Some texts were included because they supported the dominant theological or political views of the time. Others were excluded because they challenged those views. This shaping of the canon shows how much human interests have influenced not only what people believe but also what they even have the opportunity to believe.

Even the way religious texts are translated and interpreted today reflects human interests. Language changes over time, and so does the way people understand the words and ideas in these texts. Translators and scholars bring their own perspectives and priorities to their work, which can affect how the texts are understood. This is not always intentional, but it underscores how much religion is shaped by human hands and minds.

Religious practices have also been adapted to fit the needs of different societies and times. Practices that were once central to a faith may be abandoned or reinterpreted as circumstances change. New practices emerge to address modern issues. This constant evolution shows how deeply human interests are involved in religion. It also highlights the creative and resilient ways people use religion to make sense of their lives.

While these influences might seem like a problem for those seeking divine truth, they also reveal something important about religion. It is not just about reaching up to the divine. It is also about how we live together, how we build communities, and how we make meaning out of our experiences. Human interests are not something separate from religion. They are part of what makes it so dynamic and enduring. The challenge is to be honest about these influences and to approach religious texts and practices with both respect and critical awareness.

The Creation Story

The creation story is one of the most well-known parts of biblical mythology. It is a foundational tale that speaks to the origins of life, humanity, and the world itself. The story found in Genesis has been told and retold countless times, but it has also been interpreted and shaped by human hands in ways that reveal a lot about the societies and individuals engaging with it.

In its original form, the creation story presents a poetic and orderly account of how god brings the universe into existence. Light, land, water, plants, animals, and humans are created in a deliberate sequence, with each phase building upon the last. The repetition of phrases like "And god saw that it was good" gives the story a rhythm and an emphasis on the inherent value of creation. Humans are described as being made in the image of god, setting them apart as stewards of the earth. The narrative suggests harmony between god, humanity, and nature.

When we look at the story as it was originally written, it is tempting to see it as a straightforward account of divine wisdom. Yet even this version reflects human influence. The creation story, like much of biblical mythology, borrows from earlier traditions. Similar stories of creation appear in the mythologies of Mesopotamia, particularly in texts like the Enuma Elish. These earlier stories also describe a divine being organizing chaos into order, though often with more conflict and drama. The Genesis account simplifies and adapts these ideas, reflecting the monotheistic beliefs and moral priorities of the Israelites.

As the creation story was passed down, it became a canvas for interpretation. Over time, people have added layers of meaning to the text to fit their own views of the world. Early Jewish and Christian scholars debated the significance of the six-day structure. Was it meant to be taken literally, or was it symbolic? Some saw it as a precise timeline, while others viewed it as a metaphor for divine intention and creativity. These debates often reflected broader human concerns about the nature of time, science, and god's involvement in the world.

During the Middle Ages, the creation story was often interpreted in a way that reinforced the hierarchical structure of society. The idea that humans were created last, as the pinnacle of creation, was used to justify human dominance over nature. Within human societies, this logic extended to justify the dominance of certain groups over others, particularly men over women. The creation of Eve from Adam's rib became a justification for viewing women as subordinate. These interpretations say more about medieval social norms than they do about the text itself.

In more recent times, the creation story has been caught in the crossfire of debates between religion and science. Some have insisted on reading the story as a literal account, opposing scientific theories like evolution. This approach often stems from a desire to preserve the authority of biblical mythology in a modern world that increasingly values empirical evidence. On the other hand, others have embraced the creation story as a symbolic narrative, one that captures the wonder of existence without contradicting scientific discoveries. These contrasting views show how human priorities continue to shape our understanding of the text.

The creation story has also been re-imagined by various cultural and artistic movements. Writers, poets, and filmmakers have drawn on its imagery to explore themes of beginnings, relationships, and responsibility. Environmental movements have revisited the story to highlight the role of humans as caretakers of the earth, arguing that the biblical call to "subdue" the earth has been misunderstood. These reinterpretations demonstrate how flexible and enduring the creation story is, even as it is moulded by different human perspectives.

When we compare the original creation story with these many interpretations, it becomes clear that the text is not a static declaration of divine truth. It is a living narrative, one that evolves as people engage with it. The core themes of the story, creating order from chaos, the goodness of creation, and humanity's unique role remains, but the ways they are understood and applied are shaped by the times and cultures in which they are read. This ongoing process of interpretation is a reminder of how deeply human interests are woven into the fabric of religious texts and practices.

Conflicting Interpretations Of Scripture

When we dive into history, it's not hard to find examples of scripture being interpreted in conflicting ways, often because of human bias. These biases can be shaped by cultural norms, political agendas, or personal beliefs. What's fascinating is how these interpretations can vary so much that they contradict each other, even when they're supposedly based on the same text.

Take the issue of slavery in biblical mythology. For centuries, people used scripture to argue both for and against it. Those who supported slavery often pointed to verses that seemed to condone the practice, like those in Leviticus that lay out rules for owning slaves. They argued that the existence of these rules proved slavery was acceptable in the eyes of god. At the same time, abolitionists found inspiration in texts that emphasized justice, equality, and the inherent worth of all people. Passages like Galatians 3:28, which says there is neither slave nor free in Christ, were used to argue against the institution of slavery. These conflicting interpretations reveal how deeply human bias influences the way people approach scripture. The pro-slavery side often reflected economic and cultural interests, while abolitionists brought their moral and social values to the text.

Another example is the role of women in religious life. Throughout history, interpretations of biblical mythology have been used to justify both the subjugation and empowerment of women. For instance, the story of Eve's creation has often been cited as evidence that women are secondary to men, created to be their helpers. This interpretation conveniently supports patriarchal structures where men hold power. Yet others have looked at the same mythology and highlighted the shared humanity of Adam and Eve, arguing that their creation demonstrates equality. Over time, as societal attitudes toward gender roles have shifted, so have these interpretations. This shows how much cultural context shapes the way people read scripture.

The concept of "just war" is another area where conflicting interpretations emerge. Some have used biblical mythology to justify acts of war, pointing to stories where god commands battles or where wars are fought in the name of righteousness. These interpretations often reflect the political needs of the time, whether to rally troops, conquer territory, or defend against perceived enemies. On the other hand, others have focused on texts that advocate for peace and mercy, using scripture to argue against violence. These differences often boil down to the agendas of those doing the interpreting. A ruler preparing for battle might emphasize the warrior aspects of god, while a community recovering from war might lean into messages of peace.

Then there's the interpretation of wealth and poverty. Some traditions have used scripture to promote the idea that wealth is a sign of god's favour. This idea, sometimes called the "prosperity gospel," finds support in verses that describe god blessing the faithful with riches. It appeals to those who already have wealth or who aspire to it, offering divine validation for their success. On the flip side, others have focused on the numerous passages that warn against the dangers of greed and emphasize care for the poor. They argue that scripture calls for humility and generosity, not the accumulation of wealth. These conflicting interpretations often reflect economic divides, with each side finding justification for their position in the same texts.

Human bias is especially evident in how scripture has been used to justify colonization. European powers during the age of exploration often cited biblical mythology to defend their expansion into other lands. They saw themselves as bringing civilization and Christianity to "heathen" populations, interpreting their conquests as a divine mandate. At the same time, colonized peoples have used scripture to resist oppression, drawing on themes of liberation and justice. These opposing readings highlight how scripture can be wielded as a tool for both domination and resistance, depending on who is doing the interpreting.

What all these examples have in common is that they reflect the values, goals, and prejudices of the people interpreting the text. Scripture, far from being a fixed and unchanging guide, becomes a mirror that reflects the priorities of those who approach it. The same text can be twisted to support entirely different ideas, not because the words themselves change, but because human bias shapes how they are understood. This makes it clear that separating divine wisdom from human interests is no easy task.

Applying Logic And Reason To Understand Biblical Mythology

When we take a step back and apply historical research and academic inquiry to biblical mythology, we start to see it less as a divine monolith and more as a tapestry of human experience, culture, and belief. This approach doesn't seek to strip away meaning or value. Instead, it helps us understand how and why certain stories, teachings, and laws came to be. It's like uncovering the layers of a painting, where each layer tells its own story and sheds light on the choices of the artist.

One of the first things we learn from historical research is that biblical mythology wasn't created in a vacuum. The cultures surrounding the ancient Israelites heavily influenced the development of their myths and laws. For example, the creation story in Genesis has clear parallels with the Babylonian creation myth, the Enuma Elish. Both involve chaos being subdued and order established by a central deity. The key difference is how the biblical version focuses on a single god, reflecting the Israelites' monotheistic beliefs. When we recognize this connection, it becomes easier to see the Genesis creation story not as a uniquely divine account, but as one shaped by the theological needs of its time and place.

Historical analysis also shows how biblical mythology evolved over centuries. Take the laws in the Torah. Many of these laws, like those governing purity, diet, or justice, reflect the practical needs of an ancient, agrarian society. They were written to address specific issues of health, survival, and community cohesion. For instance, prohibitions against eating pork might have been tied to the risks of disease in a hot climate without refrigeration. Over time, these practical rules became spiritualized, and their original context was forgotten or reinterpreted. By studying the historical circumstances in which these laws were written, we can better understand their purpose and evaluate whether they hold relevance for modern life.

Another key area where academic inquiry helps is in understanding the political influences on biblical mythology. Many of the narratives about kings and prophets, like those in the books of Samuel or Kings, were written or edited during times of political upheaval. These stories often reflect the agendas of those in power. For example, the portrayal of King David as a flawed but ultimately chosen leader serves to legitimize his dynasty, despite his many moral failings. Similarly, the writings of prophets like Isaiah often criticize corrupt leadership while holding out hope for a future restoration. Historical research allows us to see these texts as responses to the political and social challenges of their time.

Academic inquiry also highlights the diversity of perspectives within biblical mythology. This isn't a single, unified book, but a collection of texts written by different authors with different agendas. Sometimes, these perspectives clash. The laws in Deuteronomy emphasize centralizing worship in Jerusalem, while earlier texts, like those in Judges, reflect a more decentralized form of worship. These differences reveal the tensions between various groups within ancient Israelite society. Understanding these conflicts helps us see biblical mythology as a record of human struggle and compromise, rather than a seamless expression of divine will.

The tools of archaeology and linguistics give us even more insight. Archaeological discoveries have shown that the Israelites were not a distinct group that came from outside the land of Canaan, but rather an offshoot of the Canaanite culture. This challenges the biblical narrative of conquest and instead suggests a more gradual cultural and religious evolution. Linguistic studies, meanwhile, reveal how the language of biblical mythology reflects its context. Words and phrases often have meanings tied to their time, and understanding those meanings helps us interpret the text more accurately.

By applying historical research and academic inquiry, we begin to see biblical mythology not as sacred texts, but as a collection of mythology. This doesn't diminish its value. If anything, it makes it richer and more relatable. It reminds us that the people who wrote these stories were grappling with many of the same questions we face today. How do we live ethically? How do we build a just society? How do we understand our place in the universe? These questions, shaped by their historical context, still resonate with us now.

Modern Archaeology And Biblical Mythology

Modern archaeology has been a game changer in the way we understand biblical mythology. By digging into the physical remnants of ancient civilizations, we can see where traditional interpretations of these stories hold up and where they start to crumble. What we often find is that the line between fact and myth isn't as clear as we might like. Archaeological discoveries don't just challenge traditional beliefs; they also provide context and insight into how these stories were shaped by real events, cultures, and historical shifts.

One of the most famous examples comes from the story of the Exodus. The traditional account describes a large-scale migration of Israelites from Egypt, complete with dramatic plagues and a miraculous parting of the Red Sea. For centuries, this story was taken as historical fact. But archaeological studies of the Sinai Peninsula, where the Israelites were said to wander for forty years, haven't found any evidence of a massive population travelling or settling there during the supposed time period. There are no signs of encampments, no artifacts, nothing to suggest that this event happened as described. This has led scholars to question whether the Exodus is more of a foundational myth than a historical record. That doesn't mean the story is meaningless. It could represent a collective memory of smaller migrations or reflect cultural ideas about freedom and identity that were important to the people who told it.

Jericho offers another interesting case. The biblical story of Joshua describes how the walls of Jericho fell after the Israelites marched around the city and blew their trumpets. Archaeologists have found ruins of ancient Jericho, and they've confirmed that the city's walls did collapse at some point. But the timing doesn't match up with the biblical chronology. The destruction seems to have occurred centuries before the Israelites are said to have arrived. This suggests that the story may have been adapted or borrowed from older accounts of the city's history. It might have been a way to give the Israelites a heroic origin story, tying them to a dramatic event that people in the region would have remembered.

On the other hand, there are discoveries that support certain aspects of biblical mythology. For instance, the House of David inscription found at Tel Dan is one of the first pieces of evidence outside biblical texts to reference King David. This suggests that David wasn't just a mythical figure but was likely a real leader whose life became the stuff of legend. Similarly, the ruins of ancient cities like Megiddo and Hazor show signs of destruction that align with the biblical accounts of conquests, although the causes of those destructions remain debated. These findings don't prove the stories in detail, but they do show that they're tied to real places and events.

Archaeology has also helped us understand religious practices described in biblical mythology. Excavations at ancient temples and altars often reveal objects associated with polytheistic worship, including idols of gods and goddesses. This challenges the idea that the Israelites were strictly monotheistic from the start. Instead, it suggests a gradual shift from polytheism to monotheism, with earlier Israelites likely worshipping a pantheon that included Yahweh as one deity among many. This complicates the traditional narrative but also helps us see how monotheism developed over time.

Scientific analysis of ancient texts has also played a role. For example, studies of the Dead Sea Scrolls have shown how biblical texts were copied, edited, and sometimes rewritten over centuries. This isn't just a matter of preserving words; it's a window into how beliefs and stories evolved. The scrolls reveal variations in the texts that challenge the idea of a fixed, unchanging scripture. Instead, they show a dynamic tradition where stories and teachings were shaped by the needs and ideas of different communities.

Even small details can shed light on the past. The study of ancient diets, for example, has helped us understand dietary laws in biblical mythology. Analysis of animal bones and plant remains shows what people were actually eating, which helps explain why certain foods were considered unclean. These laws weren't just spiritual but were tied to practical concerns about health, scarcity, and cultural identity.

Modern archaeology doesn't always provide simple answers, but that's part of what makes it valuable. It allows us to move beyond literal interpretations and explore the deeper layers of these stories. By uncovering the world in which biblical mythology was written, archaeology helps us appreciate these texts not just as sacred writings but as reflections of real human experiences and struggles. This perspective doesn't weaken their significance. It gives us a richer, more nuanced understanding of what they meant to the people who first told them and what they can mean to us now.

Reconciling Faith With Reason

Logic, reason, and facts are often seen as tools that challenge religious belief, but I think they can do the opposite. They have the potential to deepen and strengthen faith, making it more meaningful and resilient. Faith that stands on its own without questioning or exploration can feel fragile. It risks being shaken when confronted with evidence or ideas that don't fit neatly into its framework. But when faith is paired with logic and a willingness to explore, it becomes something stronger. It transforms into a belief system that isn't afraid to face hard questions or dig deep into the unknown.

For me, logic and reason act as a kind of compass. They help navigate the often complex terrain of religious ideas, separating the pieces that resonate with wisdom and truth from those that seem more tied to human interests or cultural biases. When you take the time to think critically about your beliefs, you're not abandoning them. You're showing that they matter enough to examine closely. You're treating them like something worth understanding fully instead of something to simply accept without thought.

Facts are just as important. They give us a grounding point, a way to anchor faith in the reality of the world we live in. Some people worry that science or evidence might disprove their beliefs, but I see it differently. The truth should never feel threatening to faith. If anything, facts give us the chance to see how our beliefs align with the way the world actually works. This alignment can be incredibly affirming. When religious ideas reflect real principles of justice, compassion, or community-building, it shows that these beliefs are about more than just abstract doctrine. They're practical and meaningful in everyday life.

Reconciliation between faith and rational inquiry is critical because it builds a bridge between belief and understanding. When faith closes itself off from logic, it risks becoming dogmatic. It stops being about searching for truth and becomes about defending itself against any kind of scrutiny. That kind of faith can feel shallow, like it's afraid of being tested. On the other hand, a faith that embraces inquiry and analysis becomes richer. It grows with the person holding it, evolving as they learn and experience more of the world.

I think it's important to understand that this process doesn't have to feel like a battle between faith and reason. They're not opposites. They're tools that work best together. Reason helps us interpret and understand our beliefs. It keeps us from getting stuck in ideas that don't make sense or don't serve us well. At the same time, faith brings something to reason that logic on its own can't provide. It gives us a sense of purpose and direction, something to aim for beyond what we can see or measure.

One of the best things about reconciling faith with reason is that it creates space for humility. When we recognize that no single person or institution has all the answers, it opens the door to continual growth and learning. It keeps us from becoming rigid in our thinking. It reminds us that wisdom is something we pursue, not something we possess. This approach doesn't weaken faith. It gives it the flexibility and strength to endure change and challenge.

Using logic, reason, and facts doesn't mean trying to explain away every mystery. It's about embracing the mystery while also seeking to understand as much as we can. Faith doesn't have to be blind to be real. It can walk hand in hand with knowledge, each one enriching the other. This way, faith becomes more than belief. It becomes a journey toward deeper truth, guided by both the light of reason and the hope that lies in our hearts.

The Intersection Of Faith And Reason

When we talk about the intersection of faith and reason, it helps to think about the work of philosophers who spent their lives exploring similar questions. Aristotle, for instance, was all about observation and logic. He believed that understanding the world required a methodical approach. For Aristotle, reason was the highest human faculty. He saw it as the way to uncover truths about the universe and our place in it. What I appreciate about his perspective is that it doesn't dismiss the idea of a higher power. Instead, it seeks to understand it. Aristotle's idea of the "Unmoved Mover" feels like a step toward reconciling faith with reason. He didn't see them as conflicting forces. He saw them as complementary tools for making sense of existence.

Kant, on the other hand, took a different approach. He believed that human understanding had limits. While reason was essential for navigating the world, he felt it couldn't fully grasp things like god or the soul. Kant argued that faith stepped in where reason reached its boundary. What's interesting about Kant's view is how he didn't treat faith as irrational. Instead, he saw it as a necessary part of moral life. For Kant, faith was what allowed us to believe in justice and the idea that doing good mattered in a larger, almost cosmic sense. His philosophy offers a kind of framework where reason takes us as far as it can, and faith carries us the rest of the way.

Hume was a skeptic. He questioned almost everything, including the idea that we could ever know anything for certain. That said, Hume didn't seem to dismiss religion outright. He was fascinated by the human tendency toward belief. Hume thought faith came from a place of emotion and experience rather than logic. While he might not have been a proponent of blending faith and reason, his ideas challenge us to think about where belief fits in the spectrum of human understanding.

Hume's work reminds us that faith isn't just about intellectual reasoning. It's deeply tied to how we experience the world.

What stands out to me about these philosophers is how they approach the same questions from such different angles. Aristotle gives us the confidence to use reason as a tool for understanding. Kant reminds us of the limits of that tool and the importance of faith in guiding our ethical lives. Hume challenges us to look at belief as something deeply human, rooted in feeling and instinct. Together, they paint a picture of faith and reason as parts of a whole rather than opposing forces.

Their work shows us that faith doesn't have to reject reason to be real, and reason doesn't have to dismiss faith to be valid. Instead, the two can inform each other. Faith can inspire reason to ask the big questions, while reason can help faith avoid getting trapped in dogma or superstition. Philosophers like Aristotle, Kant, and Hume didn't all agree, but they each explored ways that can be used to bridge the gap between what we can know and what we can believe. That exploration is where faith and reason meet. It's not about solving the mystery. It's about learning to live within it.

The Need For Reason

The need for reason, especially in the context of understanding biblical mythology, becomes apparent when we acknowledge that human beings are not perfect and are often influenced by their biases, emotions, and limited perspectives. It's easy to accept things on face value, especially when they are presented as sacred or authoritative, but without reason, we run the risk of misunderstanding or misapplying what is being communicated. Reason allows us to step back and critically engage with the text, with the goal of uncovering genuine meaning that may not be immediately obvious. It gives us the ability to question, reflect, and discern, which are essential when we're dealing with a text that has been passed down for thousands of years and has been shaped by countless human hands.

If we take a close look at biblical mythology, it's clear that reason plays an important role in how we interpret its teachings. Biblical mythology is filled with stories, symbols, and teachings that were relevant to the people who lived in ancient times, but that doesn't mean they should be accepted blindly today. Many of the ideas presented in the text reflect the culture, norms, and challenges of the people at the time of writing. These cultural contexts are different from our own, and so reason is necessary to understand how to interpret these stories in a way that resonates with our modern lives. We have to ask ourselves questions like: What was the original purpose of this teaching? How does it align with the values we hold today? And perhaps most importantly, what can we learn from it now?

Reason is also important because it helps us separate what is truly universal in biblical mythology from what is tied to specific historical contexts. There are timeless truths in biblical mythology, concepts like love, justice, and compassion, that continue to hold meaning today. However, there are also ideas that may have been culturally specific and are no longer applicable in the same way. Reason helps us distinguish between the two. For example, certain practices that were common in ancient times, like slavery or the treatment of women, are now viewed as wrong and unjust. Reason allows us to see that while these things may have been acceptable or normalized in the biblical narrative, they are not things we should emulate today.

In addition to its role in interpretation, reason is necessary for personal growth and spiritual development. Many people turn to biblical mythology for guidance in their lives. But without reason, there's the risk of becoming trapped by rigid, dogmatic thinking that doesn't allow for growth or change. A reasonable approach to biblical mythology means being open to new insights and learning from the text in ways that apply to our current lives. It's not about accepting everything without question, but about seeking a deeper understanding and using that understanding to guide our actions and our relationships with others.

Reason is also crucial in reconciling faith with the realities of the world around us. Many people struggle to see how ancient teachings can still be relevant in today's complex, scientific, and often challenging world. Without reason, it's easy to dismiss the teachings of biblical mythology as outdated or irrelevant. However, by applying reason, we can see how these teachings can be interpreted in ways that still speak to the human condition. Reason allows us to bring together faith and understanding in a way that makes sense in today's world, rather than simply accepting things on faith alone.

Lastly, reason is important because it helps us avoid the dangers of extremism. Throughout history, there have been individuals and groups who have used biblical mythology to justify harmful actions, from wars to discrimination to oppression. These people often take passages out of context or interpret them in a way that serves their own agenda. By using reason, we can guard against this. We can approach the text with a critical eye, recognizing when a passage has been twisted or misused to justify harmful actions. Reason helps us see that the true message of biblical mythology is one of love, justice, and compassion, not hatred or division.

The need for reason in understanding biblical mythology isn't about dismissing faith or tradition. It's about bringing a thoughtful, reflective approach to the text that allows us to truly understand its message and apply it in a way that is meaningful and relevant today. Reason gives us the tools to navigate the complexities of biblical mythology, and it helps us ensure that we are using its wisdom in a way that is grounded in truth and love. Without reason, we risk missing the deeper meanings that can guide us on our journey and help us live more just and compassionate lives.

The Role Of Ethics And Moral Philosophy

Ethics and moral philosophy play an essential role in helping us sort through beliefs to understand which ones genuinely contribute to our well-being and which ones cause harm. When we talk about beliefs, especially those tied to religion, it is easy to fall into the trap of thinking they are either entirely good or bad. But beliefs aren't simple. They shape how we live, how we treat others, and even how we view ourselves. This is where ethics comes in. It gives us a way to ask tough questions about the impact of a belief. Does it promote kindness? Does it encourage fairness? Does it make life better for people, or does it hurt them?

Moral philosophy takes these questions and digs even deeper. Philosophers have spent centuries asking what it means to live a good life. They've wrestled with questions about right and wrong, fairness, and the obligations we have to others. When you bring this kind of thinking into a discussion about beliefs, it opens up a space to evaluate them without dismissing them outright. It's not about attacking faith. It's about making sure the things we believe line up with the values we claim to hold.

For example, a belief that encourages people to care for the poor aligns with ethical principles found in many moral systems. It values compassion, dignity, and a sense of shared responsibility. On the other hand, a belief that justifies mistreating others based on their race, gender, or background is harmful. It contradicts the idea of fairness and respect for human worth. Ethics helps us recognize this contradiction and push back against it.

The beauty of ethics and moral philosophy is how they encourage us to think critically and empathically. They remind us to look beyond how a belief feels or what tradition says about it. Instead, they ask us to consider the real-world consequences of holding on to that belief. What happens when we live it out? Does it foster peace and understanding? Or does it create division and pain? This kind of thinking doesn't come naturally. It requires effort, honesty, and a willingness to admit when something we believe might not hold up under scrutiny.

Ethics also gives us a way to navigate disagreements about beliefs. People often hold different views about what is right or wrong, especially when it comes to religion. Moral philosophy provides a shared language to talk about those differences. It doesn't mean everyone will agree, but it creates a foundation for dialogue. It encourages us to find common ground in values like justice, compassion, and respect, even if we approach them from different angles.

At the heart of this process is the idea of accountability. Beliefs carry weight. They influence actions, policies, and relationships. When we approach them with an ethical lens, we are taking responsibility for that influence. We are saying that what we believe matters not just to us but to the people around us. This sense of accountability pushes us to choose beliefs that build up rather than tear down. It challenges us to discard harmful ideas, no matter how deeply rooted they might be.

The role of ethics and moral philosophy in examining beliefs is not to replace faith but to refine it. It is about aligning what we believe with how we want to live and how we want others to live. It is about creating a framework that allows us to distinguish between ideas that bring out the best in us and ideas that hold us back. In this way, ethics becomes a tool for growth, helping us move closer to the values we aspire to embody.

Evaluating Religious Ethics With Objective Facts

When we talk about evaluating religious ethics, especially in the context of biblical mythology, it's important to approach it with a mindset of objective reasoning and evidence-based thinking. Religious teachings, particularly those from ancient texts, have been passed down through centuries, often without being questioned. This tradition has its value, but as society progresses, it becomes necessary to scrutinize these teachings and assess their real-world impact. The goal isn't to discard faith but to ensure that the ideas we embrace are beneficial and aligned with what we know about human well-being and justice.

One of the first steps in this process is recognizing that not all teachings in biblical mythology are equally helpful today. Some ideas were relevant in their original context but have become outdated as our understanding of the world has grown. For example, many biblical teachings reflect the cultural norms of ancient societies, where issues like slavery, gender inequality, and violence were not only accepted but often institutionalized. These ideas were embedded in the moral and ethical framework of the time, but modern ethical standards, grounded in principles like equality, human dignity, and respect for individual rights, show that these interpretations no longer serve the collective good.

To evaluate biblical teachings, we need to apply the same evidence-based reasoning we use to assess any other ethical or moral principle. For instance, when we look at teachings that promote kindness, generosity, and justice, we see that they align with modern social values that encourage peace, empathy, and fairness. These are ideas that contribute positively to society and can be supported by evidence showing that compassionate, just societies tend to thrive and foster well-being for their citizens. In contrast, teachings that justify harm or discrimination, even if they are rooted in tradition, should be questioned. Just because a belief has historical significance doesn't mean it is right or helpful today.

Using objective facts to assess these teachings means considering the real-world consequences of holding onto them. Take, for example, teachings that have been used to justify discrimination against certain groups of people, whether based on gender, race, or sexuality. These interpretations have caused harm for generations. Objective reasoning, supported by evidence from fields like sociology, psychology, and history, demonstrates that societies that embrace diversity and equality tend to have stronger, healthier communities. The benefits of inclusion, respect, and equal treatment are well-documented, and these are the principles we should support when evaluating religious ethics.

By applying this type of reasoning, we can discard harmful interpretations that serve the interests of those in power but do not promote the greater good. This isn't about rejecting religious texts but about separating the timeless wisdom they may contain from the outdated ideas that have been inserted over time. It is about moving beyond literal interpretations that serve patriarchal or authoritarian structures and focusing on the values that promote universal well-being. We can keep the core teachings that encourage love, peace, and justice, while letting go of those that perpetuate harm.

This process requires us to be honest with ourselves about the harmful effects of certain beliefs, even when they are wrapped in religious authority. It also requires us to acknowledge that our understanding of morality has evolved, and with it, our ability to make decisions that lead to better outcomes for everyone. Evidence-based reasoning isn't just a tool for science; it is a way of ensuring that the beliefs we hold, especially those tied to ethics and morality, continue to serve us well as individuals and as a society.

In the end, evaluating religious ethics with objective facts is about improving the way we live together. It's about using the knowledge we have accumulated through reason, science, and human experience to guide our beliefs and practices. By discarding harmful or outdated teachings and focusing on those that promote human flourishing, we can ensure that our ethical frameworks remain relevant, just, and compassionate.

Re-evaluating Religious Doctrines

Re-evaluating religious doctrines is a challenging but necessary step for anyone seeking to deepen their faith while also aligning it with truth and reason. Many religious doctrines, particularly those tied to biblical mythology, have been passed down through centuries, often with layers of human bias attached to them. These biases can obscure the original, divine wisdom that might have been embedded in the teachings. Eidotheosophy offers a way to re-evaluate these doctrines by encouraging believers to seek the divine wisdom that transcends human distortion. By applying its principles, believers can engage in a more meaningful and transformative practice of faith.

To apply the principles of eidotheosophy to faith practice, believers need to be willing to step back and critically assess their beliefs. This process involves recognizing that human biases, cultural influences, and historical contexts have shaped the way religious teachings have been interpreted. These biases often serve particular interests, whether they are political, social, or cultural. In the context of eidotheosophy, the goal is to strip away these layers of distortion and return to a more direct understanding of divine wisdom. This doesn't mean abandoning religious beliefs, but it requires a shift in focus from dogma and tradition to a deeper connection with what is truly beneficial for human flourishing.

One way believers can begin this process is by reflecting on the core values of their faith and evaluating them in light of modern understanding. The divine wisdom that may be present in religious teachings is often centered around love, compassion, justice, and peace. These principles can be applied in everyday life to guide personal decisions and interactions with others. By focusing on these universal values, believers can shift their focus away from rigid interpretations or practices that may no longer serve the greater good and instead embrace a more compassionate, justice-oriented practice of faith.

This process also involves being open to the idea that some religious doctrines, while meaningful in their original context, may no longer be relevant or helpful today. For example, teachings that have been used to justify harm, exclusion, or inequality should be re-examined through the lens of eidotheosophy. These doctrines might have served a particular purpose in the past, but as society evolves, it becomes clear that they don't align with the broader, more inclusive vision of love and justice that many faiths advocate. Re-evaluating these doctrines involves being willing to discard them when they are found to be harmful, outdated, or inconsistent with the values that promote human well-being.

The challenge of discarding human biases is particularly difficult because many of these biases are deeply ingrained in our religious practices and community structures. They often come from longstanding traditions and interpretations that have shaped our understanding of spirituality. However, the process of re-evaluating religious doctrines with the principles of eidotheosophy involves being honest about the human influence on our beliefs and recognizing that divine wisdom is not bound by tradition or human institutions. By embracing a more open, flexible approach to faith, believers can reconnect with the deeper, universal truths that lie at the heart of their religion.

At the same time, applying eidotheosophy doesn't require rejecting faith or spirituality. Rather, it encourages a deeper, more thoughtful engagement with these concepts. It's about finding the divine wisdom in the teachings and applying it in ways that make sense for the world today. In this way, the practice of faith becomes not just a set of rituals or beliefs, but a living, breathing part of one's daily life. It becomes a tool for personal growth, social justice, and collective well-being, shaped by both divine wisdom and the thoughtful application of reason.

Ultimately, re-evaluating religious doctrines through the lens of eidotheosophy allows believers to deepen their faith while also ensuring that their beliefs are aligned with the principles that promote peace, compassion, and justice. It's a process of continuous reflection, learning, and growth, one that keeps faith relevant and beneficial in an ever-changing world. By discarding human biases and focusing on divine wisdom, believers can create a more inclusive, loving, and just practice of faith that truly embodies the best of their spiritual traditions.

Eidotheosophy And The Metaphysical Elements Of Biblical Mythology

The metaphysical elements of biblical mythology are a fascinating and deeply personal aspect of faith that sits at the edges of what we can understand and discuss in practical terms. Eidotheosophy focuses on separating divine wisdom from human invention in a way that is grounded in reason and evidence, but it does not extend into metaphysical concepts like the nature of god, Christ, other spiritual beings, or the afterlife. These ideas are inherently untestable and exist outside the scope of our current understanding of reality. That doesn't mean they lack value or meaning; it just means they aren't something we can evaluate with the same tools we use to understand more tangible aspects of faith and life.

When it comes to metaphysical concepts, there is always the possibility that divine wisdom could reveal these truths through the influence of the holy spirit. Many believers speak of personal revelations, moments of spiritual clarity, or encounters that feel like direct communication from god. These experiences are often deeply moving and transformative, and they shape how individuals understand metaphysical questions. However, because such moments are subjective, they can't be tested or confirmed in a way that makes them universally applicable. What feels like divine revelation to one person might seem like imagination or coincidence to another. That doesn't make these experiences any less real for the person who has them, but it does highlight the limits of what we can assert with confidence.

The difficulty in distinguishing whether these metaphysical ideas arise from human creativity or divine influence is part of what makes them so enduring. Humans have always been storytellers, and much of what we find in biblical mythology reflects the hopes, fears, and questions that have shaped our collective imagination. The concept of an afterlife, for example, speaks to our longing for justice, our fear of mortality, and our desire to be reunited with those we've lost. Similarly, ideas about the nature of god or spiritual entities often reflect the qualities we most value, those of love, power, wisdom, and justice. It's entirely possible that these ideas are inspired by divine wisdom, filtered through the lens of human understanding, or that they are entirely human constructs created to make sense of the unknown. There is no way to definitively say.

What is clear is that these metaphysical components of biblical mythology have a profound impact on how people live their lives. They inspire acts of great kindness and courage, as well as moments of reflection and wonder. They can also lead to division and conflict when differing interpretations clash. This dual potential underscores why these ideas should be approached with humility. We don't know if they are true, but we also can't dismiss them outright. The best we can do is hold them with an open mind, recognizing that they might contain pieces of divine wisdom or simply reflect our human attempts to grapple with the mysteries of existence.

In acknowledging the limits of what we can know, eidotheosophy aims to focus on what is actionable and meaningful in our shared human experience. Whether or not the metaphysical ideas in biblical mythology come from god, they invite us to ask questions that are deeply important, ideas about the nature of good and evil, the meaning of life, and what it means to be in relationship with the divine. These questions may not have definitive answers, but they push us to think deeply and live thoughtfully. For now, that may be the most valuable thing they offer.

The Plain Meaning Interpretation

The plain meaning interpretation is one of the most straightforward ways to approach biblical mythology, but it's also one of the most commonly misunderstood. It essentially means taking the text at face value, reading it for what it says directly without trying to read between the lines or overcomplicate things. It's the idea that the words on the page, in their simplest form, communicate the message that god intended. On the surface, this sounds simple enough, but when it comes to ancient texts like biblical mythology, things aren't always as clear as they seem.

When we talk about the plain meaning, we're talking about the text itself, without jumping into allegory or deeper, symbolic interpretations right away. For example, if a story in biblical mythology talks about someone parting a sea or raising the dead, the plain meaning interpretation would focus on what these events directly tell us about the people, the time, and the message. This doesn't mean we ignore the possibility of metaphor or symbolism, but we start with what's right in front of us. It's kind of like hearing a story from a friend and simply listening to the words, without immediately assuming they're hiding some deeper truth. You hear it as it is, first and foremost.

The reason this approach is important is that sometimes, in an effort to understand or explain the text, people can get so caught up in finding hidden meanings or symbolic layers that they overlook the core message that's right there. When we engage with the plain meaning interpretation, we get to experience the text as it was presented to its original audience. This can help ground us in the context and history, allowing us to better understand why these stories were told in the first place. We may also realize that while there may be hidden meanings or deeper symbols, the most important messages in biblical mythology are often the simplest ones.

Of course, it's not as easy as just reading the text and saying, "This is what it means." Biblical mythology was written in a very different time, and the language used in the text reflects the culture, beliefs, and practices of that era. So, while the plain meaning interpretation can give us a starting point, it's still important to understand the historical and cultural background. For example, when we read about miracles or divine acts, we need to consider what those actions meant to the people of that time. Their understanding of the world was different from ours, so the plain meaning might be a little less straightforward than we might expect.

The plain meaning interpretation also helps us avoid overcomplicating things. When we start getting too caught up in complex theories or endless interpretations, we risk losing sight of the very things that make biblical mythology so powerful. The stories are meant to teach us lessons, give us guidance, and help us understand our place in the world and with god. When we interpret them in ways that are overly complicated or abstract, we might miss out on the simple, direct wisdom that's there for us to apply in our lives.

There's also something humbling about the plain meaning interpretation. It encourages us to approach biblical mythology with a certain kind of openness, a willingness to take it for what it is without needing to constantly analyze or justify it. We don't have to make everything fit into a neat, intellectual box. Sometimes, the stories in biblical mythology speak for themselves, and by embracing their plain meaning, we allow ourselves to just listen. In doing so, we open up the possibility of applying the lessons of the text more directly to our own lives.

Another aspect of the plain meaning interpretation is that it allows the text to be accessible to everyone. When we start diving too deep into allegorical interpretations or complicated theological ideas, the text can become something only scholars or experts can understand. But by focusing on the plain meaning, we make biblical mythology something that anyone can engage with. It's not about needing specialized knowledge or complex analysis to get the message. It's about opening the text up to all people, allowing its wisdom to be understood by anyone who is willing to listen.

However, that's not to say the plain meaning interpretation is without its challenges. When we approach the text literally, we also have to confront some of the more difficult aspects of biblical mythology, especially the parts that may seem outdated or even troubling by modern standards. Things like violence, discrimination, and other practices that were once common but are no longer acceptable in the same way can be jarring when read at face value. But this is where understanding the historical context becomes essential. The plain meaning is a starting point, but we need to consider the time and place where the story was told. That doesn't excuse harmful actions, but it helps us understand why they were included in the first place and how they fit into the larger narrative.

In the end, the plain meaning interpretation is about recognizing the power of simplicity. It's about reading biblical mythology with an open heart and mind, ready to hear the message as it is given, without overcomplicating things. It doesn't mean ignoring deeper meanings, but it does mean allowing the text to speak directly to us in a way that's clear and understandable. It's a reminder that sometimes the simplest interpretations hold the most profound truths, and in the case of biblical mythology, that can be a powerful way to engage with the stories that have shaped so much of human history.

Avoiding Hidden Meanings Or Esoteric Interpretations

When it comes to understanding biblical mythology, there's a tendency to get lost in the search for hidden meanings or esoteric interpretations. We often hear people say that the text isn't just about what it says on the surface, that there's a deeper, secret meaning waiting to be unlocked by only the most knowledgeable or spiritually enlightened. While there's certainly room for symbolism and deeper understanding, I think it's important to be cautious about jumping too quickly into these interpretations. Sometimes, in our eagerness to find something more profound, we overlook the beauty and clarity of the text as it stands.

The first thing to keep in mind is that the simple, plain meaning of the stories in biblical mythology often carries a lot of weight. These stories were told to convey important lessons about life, god, and human nature. It's easy to assume that there's always more beneath the surface, but by doing so, we might miss the basic wisdom that's meant to be understood by everyone. The stories of biblical mythology were never meant to be a puzzle with layers of hidden truths that only a select few could unlock. They were meant to be passed down, understood, and applied to daily life, by people in all walks of life.

When we get too caught up in hidden meanings or esoteric readings, we start to complicate the message. Take, for example, some of the miraculous events described in biblical mythology, like the parting of the Red Sea or the resurrection of the dead. There's no denying that these events are extraordinary, but when we get obsessed with trying to find a secret code or metaphor that explains everything, we lose sight of the power of those moments. They serve a purpose, one that is deeply tied to the message being conveyed at the time. The parting of the Red Sea, for instance, is about deliverance and divine intervention at a crucial moment in history, not necessarily about an allegory of something else. Sometimes, the most direct interpretation is the most meaningful.

I also think we have to be careful of allowing our own biases to shape our understanding of hidden meanings. It's easy to read into a story based on what we want it to mean, especially if we're looking for something that aligns with our own beliefs or experiences. This is where esoteric interpretations can get dangerous. They can distort the text in a way that serves our own interests, rather than allowing the text to speak for itself. If we constantly look for hidden meanings or secret codes that confirm our preexisting views, we're not really engaging with the text honestly. Instead, we're just projecting our own ideas onto it.

Part of avoiding esoteric interpretations also comes from understanding the context in which biblical mythology was written. These stories were told to people living in a specific time and place, with certain cultural and historical circumstances that influenced how they understood the world. The meaning of a story made sense to them because they had the same worldview and the same understanding of life, nature, and the divine. We, on the other hand, are separated by thousands of years of cultural change. It's tempting to try to make the text fit into our modern understanding, but we have to remember that it was never intended to be decoded in the same way. The people who first heard these stories didn't have the benefit of centuries of theological study and philosophy. They understood the stories in a much more immediate way.

There's also the issue of selective interpretation. When we begin looking for hidden meanings, we often ignore parts of the text that don't fit into our desired interpretation. We might focus on specific symbols, numbers, or words that seem mysterious, but in doing so, we might miss other parts of the text that offer more straightforward and useful guidance. It's easy to get lost in the idea of "decoding" the text, but this can lead us to cherry-pick the bits that support our ideas while dismissing those that don't. This selective reading creates a skewed understanding of biblical mythology, one that's shaped more by our personal desires than by the text itself.

What I believe is crucial to remember is that, while there's always room for thoughtful reflection and deeper layers of meaning, we shouldn't lose sight of the primary purpose of biblical mythology: to offer lessons that are accessible, clear, and universally applicable. Hidden meanings are often an excuse to create a more complex, intellectual version of the text that may be more about showing off knowledge than truly understanding what's being said. The real power of the biblical stories comes from their ability to speak directly to us, to offer insights into our lives without needing to veil those insights in secrecy.

By avoiding the temptation to constantly search for hidden meanings or secret knowledge, we allow the text to be something that speaks to everyone, not just those who think they have the key to unlock its mysteries. The more we focus on the simple meaning, the clearer the message becomes. The biblical stories are about love, justice, compassion, and understanding. They're meant to guide us in our lives, not to keep us guessing about some hidden truth. When we remove the need for esoteric interpretations, we make the text something that can be shared and applied across time and space, without needing to complicate its basic wisdom.

Biblical mythology Is Not Literally The Word Of god

The idea that biblical mythology is literally the word of god is one of those beliefs that has been held for centuries, but when you really take a step back and look at the history of how the text was formed, it's clear that it doesn't line up with that concept in a straightforward way. People often say that every word of biblical mythology is directly dictated by god, but when you examine the text closely, you see a much more complex process at play. biblical mythology, as we know it, is a collection of writings, many of which were written by various human authors over a long period of time, reflecting their own perspectives, beliefs, and cultural influences. It wasn't handed down on a golden tablet or written in a single moment of divine inspiration.

One of the first things to understand is that biblical mythology, especially when we refer to it as biblical mythology, has been passed down through many different generations and cultures. The stories contained within it evolved over time, sometimes being reinterpreted and edited to suit the needs of the people who were living at the time. The fact that it was written by humans, over centuries, in different languages, and from different social and political contexts, already calls into question the idea of it being literally the word of god. If it was truly the literal word of god, we would expect it to be a perfect and consistent message. Instead, we see different styles of writing, different perspectives, and even contradictions within the text. These are signs that biblical mythology is not a single, uniform message directly from a divine source, but rather a complex collection of human writings.

One of the most significant aspects of biblical mythology is that it reflects the cultural and historical context in which it was written. The ideas, laws, and beliefs presented in biblical mythology often reflect the norms of the time, and many of them are tied to the experiences and challenges that the people of ancient Israel and surrounding areas faced. For instance, the concept of a god who demands loyalty and obedience can be seen as part of the political and social structure of the ancient world, where kings and rulers often used religion as a tool for maintaining control. If we see biblical mythology as a reflection of those times, rather than a literal, unchanging word of god, it starts to make more sense. biblical mythology wasn't just dropped from the heavens; it was shaped by the human beings who wrote it, influenced by their own understanding of the world and their relationship with god.

Even within the text itself, we see evidence that biblical mythology is not meant to be taken literally in every sense. Take the parables, for example. Jesus' teachings, especially in the gospels, are full of stories that are not meant to be understood as literal truths, but rather as lessons about human nature and god's will. These are stories told to illustrate moral and spiritual truths, not to convey historical or factual events. If we understand biblical mythology as containing these kinds of stories, alongside historical accounts and laws, it becomes clear that not everything in it is meant to be taken literally. biblical mythology functions as a tool for understanding our relationship with god, with others, and with the world, but it doesn't require us to believe that every word is a literal, divine command.

The process of canonization also plays a significant role in how we think about biblical mythology. biblical mythology as we have it today is the result of a long process of selecting certain books and writings and excluding others. Early Christians and Jewish scholars had to decide which texts were authoritative and which were not, a decision that was made based on theological, political, and cultural considerations. If biblical mythology was literally the word of god, we wouldn't need a process like this to decide what belongs and what doesn't. The very fact that there were debates, disagreements, and revisions shows that biblical mythology was shaped by human hands.

These decisions were made by people, not by some divine force dictating the text to them.

One of the more challenging aspects of viewing biblical mythology as literally the word of god is the moral issues it presents. Many parts of biblical mythology contain laws and commands that, by today's standards, would be considered unethical or even downright immoral. For example, there are passages that endorse slavery, violence, and the subjugation of women. If we were to insist that biblical mythology is literally the word of god, we would have to accept these ideas as divine commands. However, when we acknowledge the historical and cultural context of these writings, we can see that these are reflections of the time in which they were written, not timeless divine laws. The moral teachings in biblical mythology are important, but they must be understood in the context of the people who wrote them, and not as an unchanging command from god.

In the end, biblical mythology is a product of its time, shaped by human hands and human understanding. It is not a literal transcript of god speaking directly to us, but rather a collection of texts that reflect the beliefs, struggles, and insights of the people who wrote them. By understanding biblical mythology in this way, we can engage with it more honestly and thoughtfully. We can appreciate the wisdom it offers without feeling the need to interpret every word as if it came straight from the mouth of god. Instead of looking for a literal word of god, we can look at biblical mythology as a record of humanity's attempts to understand the divine, and in doing so, we can find meaning and guidance for our own lives.

What Is The Word Of god?

The concept of the "word of god" is one that has been debated and discussed for centuries, often leading to a lot of confusion and differing interpretations. For many people, the word of god is thought of as a literal and divine message, often equated with biblical mythology or a specific set of texts that are seen as direct revelations from god. But when you look at biblical mythology and consider the broader context of how these texts were created, it becomes clear that the word of god isn't as straightforward as many people imagine it to be.

First, we need to think about what it means to communicate. Communication is not just about words on a page or phrases spoken aloud. It's about transmitting ideas, emotions, and experiences. In the biblical context, the "word" often isn't about a specific phrase or commandment, but rather about a relationship or interaction. When we think of god speaking in biblical mythology, it's often not just about dictating rules or laws; it's about expressing something deeper, something that reflects the nature of god and the divine will for humanity. The word of god, in this sense, is not just about the literal text; it's about the deeper meaning that these words convey. biblical mythology is full of messages that convey moral guidance, justice, love, and the nature of human relationships with god and with each other. This broader understanding of god's word is much more than a set of written instructions. It's an invitation to live in harmony with god's will.

In biblical mythology, god's word is often portrayed as a force of creation. In the very first chapter of Genesis, we see god speaking the world into existence. "Let there be light" is not just a simple command, it's an expression of divine power that brings about change and order. In this context, the word of god is not just a statement or a command, but an active, creative force. It's not something that simply exists in the pages of a book, but something that has the power to shape and transform reality. The word of god is a dynamic, living force that has the ability to create, heal, and bring life. It's not limited to the written word; it is also embodied in the actions, teachings, and presence of god as experienced by those who follow the divine path.

Throughout biblical mythology, we also see that god's word is often revealed through individuals who speak on god's behalf. The prophets, for instance, are considered to be the messengers of god's word. These figures are not merely reading from a script; they are receiving divine inspiration and conveying that message to the people. They are acting as intermediaries, taking the word of god and interpreting it for those who might not be able to understand it directly. This is why the word of god is sometimes portrayed as something that can be experienced through human beings, through their actions, words, and lives. It's not just about receiving a written text, but about living according to god's will and passing that understanding on to others.

The teachings of Jesus, as portrayed in the gospels, offer another perspective on the word of god. In many ways, Jesus himself is described as the living word of god. His actions, his teachings, and his very being are an embodiment of god's will on earth. He doesn't just speak about god's kingdom; he demonstrates it through his life, his interactions with others, and his willingness to sacrifice himself. The word of god, in this sense, isn't just a message written down for future generations, it's something that can be seen and experienced in the lives of those who follow god's path. It's not a static set of rules; it's a living, breathing presence that continues to manifest in the world around us.

Another aspect of the word of god is its relationship to wisdom. In many parts of biblical mythology, wisdom is personified as a woman, as seen in the book of Proverbs. This personification of wisdom emphasizes that god's word is not just about following rules or commandments, but about seeking understanding, insight, and discernment. It's about cultivating a deeper relationship with the divine and seeking to live in a way that reflects that understanding. Wisdom is not just about intellectual knowledge; it's about living in a way that aligns with god's will and reflects the goodness and truth that comes from that relationship.

In the context of eidotheosophy, we can think of the word of god as a bridge between the divine and human experience. It's not about taking every word of biblical mythology literally, but about understanding the deeper meaning behind the text and how it can guide us in our lives today. The word of god is not confined to the pages of a book; it's something that can be experienced and lived out in our daily lives. It's about embracing the divine wisdom and teachings that are woven throughout biblical mythology and using them as a compass to navigate the challenges and complexities of life. The word of god, in this sense, is not just something to be read or memorized, it's something to be understood, internalized, and applied in our lives, helping us to live in a way that reflects the love, justice, and truth that are at the heart of the divine will.

Believers Need to Research Their Own Faith Related Issues

When it comes to faith, it's essential that each believer takes responsibility for their own understanding. It's easy to rely on what we've been told or taught, especially when it comes to deep, complex issues about god, spirituality, and the teachings of biblical mythology. But simply accepting someone else's interpretation without doing the work to understand for ourselves leaves us vulnerable to manipulation or being misled. The need to research your own faith-related issues is critical. It's about becoming an active participant in your spiritual journey rather than just a passive recipient of someone else's ideas.

Biblical mythology shows us that true understanding comes from seeking knowledge. People like Jesus or the prophets never demanded blind obedience. Instead, they encouraged self-reflection, learning, and searching for deeper meaning. Even in the Old Testament, we see examples of people questioning, wrestling with their beliefs, and seeking wisdom directly from god. This was never about accepting things at face value. The message of biblical mythology consistently encourages people to ask questions and seek knowledge, not just to accept things without critically engaging with them. So, if you're not taking the time to research and understand the deeper meaning behind your faith, you're missing out on an essential part of the spiritual journey.

The danger of not researching your faith is that you can end up adopting someone else's version of the truth, which may not align with the core principles of biblical mythology. Teachers and leaders might have good intentions, but they are still human. They can be wrong or may emphasize certain aspects of the faith that serve their own agenda. The role of believers is not just to accept what is handed down to them but to actively engage with their faith in a meaningful way. Whether it's reading different interpretations of biblical texts or seeking out other religious scholars, diving deep into the faith helps you understand its nuances and how it applies to your life. Without this kind of engagement, you risk following along with the crowd, repeating what others say without really knowing why.

In many ways, this kind of personal research can be seen as an act of stewardship. Just as we're responsible for taking care of our lives, our health, or our families, we are also responsible for taking care of our spiritual understanding. We're responsible for being critical thinkers who seek out truth. And this doesn't mean rejecting authority or guidance altogether. Teachers and spiritual leaders are important, but they should be seen as guides, not as the sole source of truth. No matter how much someone may seem to know, they're still human, and their interpretation of biblical mythology may not be the only one. Each believer should strive to build their understanding based on careful, personal study and research.

One of the most profound things about biblical mythology is how it challenges us to think for ourselves. God is presented as being available to everyone, and the path to wisdom is not restricted to a chosen few. It's open to all who seek it. Biblical mythology encourages individuals to think, to question, and to engage deeply with the world around them. If we look at figures like Solomon, who prayed for wisdom, or Jesus, who constantly taught people to see beyond the surface and understand the deeper truths of the world, we see that true spirituality is about more than just following what someone else says. It's about wrestling with difficult questions, seeking answers, and striving for deeper wisdom.

Also, doing your own research on faith-related issues can help you develop a stronger and more personal connection to your beliefs. When you read, study, and understand the teachings, you are able to personalize them. It's one thing to listen to a preacher or a scholar give their take on biblical mythology. It's another to read it for yourself, reflect on it, and apply it in a way that speaks to your own experience. Each believer's journey is unique, and what resonates with one person may not resonate with another. By doing your own research, you can find the aspects of faith that truly speak to you and help you grow spiritually.

One of the challenges today is that there's so much information available, and it can be hard to know where to start. But this doesn't mean that believers should shy away from researching. There are countless resources, from biblical translations to historical research, that can help you get a better understanding of the text. And even though not everything you read will be immediately clear, the act of searching and questioning helps to clarify your own thoughts and beliefs. If you're not willing to look deeper into your own faith, you risk following a path that's shaped by someone else's perspective. You might end up with a shallow understanding of something that is meant to be transformative and life-changing.

Faith is meant to be lived out, not just thought about. It's meant to shape the way we act, how we treat others, and how we make sense of the world. By researching your faith, you gain the tools to live it out more fully. You are better equipped to deal with the challenges that come your way. Life isn't simple, and the answers to life's biggest questions are rarely easy. But that's where research comes in; when you study biblical mythology and dig deeper into what the faith really teaches, you gain a perspective that helps you navigate the complexities of life. You learn to think critically, to approach problems with wisdom, and to understand where your beliefs fit into the broader world around you. This isn't just about learning facts or memorizing verses; it's about understanding the deeper meaning behind your beliefs and how they shape who you are.

There's a certain responsibility that comes with being a believer. It's not just about attending services or following rituals; it's about actively engaging with your faith, questioning it, understanding it, and living it. And that's why research is so important. It's about taking control of your spiritual journey and making it something that is deeply meaningful to you. The more you learn and the more you research, the more you grow spiritually, and the more you can contribute to the world around you. When you take the time to understand your faith in a deep, personal way, it becomes an integral part of who you are. This kind of active engagement is what makes faith real and alive, not just something that you inherit but something you've truly embraced.

The Danger Of Blindly Following Tradition

Tradition can be a powerful thing. It's comforting and familiar, and it often carries a sense of continuity with the past. But sometimes, tradition can become a trap, especially when it's followed blindly. In the context of faith, blindly following tradition can be especially dangerous because it prevents people from thinking critically and questioning the validity of what they've been taught. In biblical mythology, there are multiple instances where traditions were upheld without understanding their deeper meaning, and those practices led people away from what god truly intended. The danger lies in treating tradition as an unquestionable authority rather than a tool to help us grow and understand our faith.

One of the problems with blindly following tradition is that it can often mask the real, genuine meanings that might be more difficult to grasp. When you rely solely on tradition, you may end up repeating rituals or adhering to beliefs without really understanding why they exist in the first place. This can result in a hollow experience, where the essence of the tradition is lost. For example, many of the rituals in biblical mythology, like sacrifices or specific laws, were meant to bring people closer to god or help them live in accordance with divine principles. Over time, however, these traditions became mere formalities, disconnected from their original purpose. People followed them because that's what they were told to do, not because they understood the deeper message behind them.

In biblical mythology, the prophets often warned about this kind of empty tradition. The religious leaders of Jesus' time were especially guilty of this. They had turned the commandments into a set of rules to be followed mechanically, without understanding the spirit of the law. Jesus himself criticized this approach, pointing out that god desired mercy, justice, and humility, not mindless adherence to traditions. By focusing too much on the letter of the law and not the heart of it, people were missing the whole point. This is exactly what happens when we blindly follow tradition. It can lead to a kind of spiritual deadness, where people go through the motions but fail to experience any real connection to the divine.

Another danger of blindly following tradition is that it can prevent growth and change. In the history of religious traditions, change is often seen as threatening. People become so attached to the way things have always been done that they resist any kind of innovation or reinterpretation. This kind of rigidity can stifle new insights and prevent us from seeing things from a different perspective. Faith, however, should be something that grows with us over time. The traditions of our faith are not meant to trap us in the past, but to guide us as we evolve and develop a deeper understanding of the world and of god. Blindly following tradition means we stop learning. We stop questioning. We stop searching for deeper truths.

Biblical mythology speaks to the importance of being able to adapt and grow in understanding. In the Old Testament, for example, god speaks to the prophets, who then speak to the people, but there's always this underlying sense that things are constantly changing. The commandments themselves evolve. God's relationship with humanity evolves. To blindly follow tradition is to miss the dynamic, living aspect of faith. The stories in biblical mythology are not static; they are about learning, growing, and transforming. They urge us to move beyond simple, rote adherence to tradition and into a more profound relationship with god and with each other.

When we talk about the danger of blindly following tradition, we also need to consider the potential harm it can cause. When tradition becomes an unquestioned authority, it can be used to justify harmful practices, discrimination, or injustice. In history, religious traditions have been used to justify wars, oppression, and persecution. People have been harmed, often in the name of protecting tradition. In biblical mythology, we see instances where traditions were used to control and marginalize certain groups of people. This is a warning to us today: when tradition is placed above human dignity or compassion, it becomes destructive. Faith should never be used as a tool for oppression, yet we see throughout history how that has happened when people became more invested in preserving tradition than in living out the true teachings of their faith.

Blindly following tradition also disconnects us from the lived experiences of others. The world is constantly changing, and people's experiences and struggles evolve. When we hold on too tightly to tradition, we risk becoming disconnected from the people around us. Biblical mythology, especially through the teachings of Jesus, constantly reminds us of the importance of empathy and compassion. It encourages us to look beyond what is traditionally accepted and to engage with people on a deeper, more human level. By not critically examining the traditions we follow, we shut ourselves off from the richness of human experience and the opportunity to learn from others.

Tradition, in and of itself, is not bad. It can be a way to pass down wisdom, create community, and provide structure. But when tradition is followed without questioning, it becomes dangerous. It stops being a tool for growth and turns into a barrier to true understanding. Biblical mythology, particularly through its stories of prophets and spiritual leaders, teaches us that traditions should be examined, reinterpreted, and understood in the context of the ever-changing world. Blindly following tradition without understanding its purpose or context not only hinders our spiritual growth but also makes it easier to be manipulated or misled. It's a reminder that faith isn't about following a set of rules; it's about building a relationship with the divine and with others. The tradition should serve that relationship, not replace it.

Biblical Laws And Traditions Were Never Meant For Non-Jewish People

When we look at biblical mythology, we see that the laws and traditions given to the people of Israel were not necessarily meant for non-Jewish people. The biblical narrative, particularly in the Old Testament, shows that these laws were designed to set the Israelites apart from other nations. The idea was that by following these laws, they would be a distinct people, chosen by god to fulfill a unique purpose in the world. The laws were never about forcing everyone to follow them, but rather about maintaining a particular identity and relationship with god. It's important to remember that the laws were, first and foremost, for the Israelites to follow.

The concept of being a chosen people is embedded deeply in the biblical story. From the time of Abraham, god sets apart the descendants of Israel, marking them with specific practices and laws to distinguish them from the surrounding nations. These laws covered everything from dietary restrictions to how they worshipped, how they interacted with one another, and even how they treated the land. These were not universal laws meant for the entire world. They were meant to help Israel remain holy and separate, following the commandments given directly to them by god. It wasn't about trying to enforce a global standard of behavior but about maintaining a special covenant with a specific people.

In fact, the very nature of many of the laws shows that they were intended to regulate the internal life of the Israelite community. The cleanliness laws, for example, and the laws around sacrifice were about helping the Israelites live in a way that would keep them set apart for god's purposes. These laws weren't meant for the people around them, nor were they a universal moral code. They were specific to a people who had been chosen to carry out god's will in the world. They weren't about imposing rules on non-Jews but about keeping Israel's relationship with god intact and distinct.

Even when we move into the New Testament, there's a shift in how the laws are applied. Jesus' teachings, as presented in the gospels, start to break down the boundaries that had previously existed. Jesus himself, in his interactions with non-Jews, showed that the old laws were not meant to be a barrier for everyone else. Instead of requiring everyone to follow the laws of the Old Testament, Jesus emphasized love, compassion, and faith. The New Testament, especially in the letters of Paul, makes it clear that the old laws were not meant for Gentiles (non-Jews). Paul teaches that faith in Christ, not adherence to the Old Testament laws, is what brings people into a relationship with god. This is a significant shift, one that reinterprets the meaning and purpose of the Old Testament laws.

When we consider the role of the early church, we see that the debate over whether non-Jews should follow the laws of Israel became a major issue. The Jerusalem Council in Acts 15 addresses this very issue, deciding that Gentile converts to Christianity were not required to follow the Mosaic laws, especially the laws of circumcision and dietary restrictions. This decision marked a crucial turning point, as it made clear that the teachings of Jesus were not about imposing Jewish laws on the broader world. Instead, they were about inviting people from all nations into a new kind of relationship with god, a relationship based on faith and love rather than ritual observance.

This shift is also reflected in the writings of the early church fathers. They made a clear distinction between the laws meant for Israel and the broader message of Christianity, which was available to all people, regardless of their background. The idea was that the laws given to the Israelites were part of a specific historical context, tied to a specific covenant. They were never intended to be a global standard for all humanity. In fact, the very nature of the covenant with Israel shows that these laws were a part of god's plan for that people at that time. They weren't meant to be a timeless, universal set of moral principles for all people to follow.

One of the dangers of misinterpreting these laws is that it can lead to a misunderstanding of the role of Christianity in the world. If we mistakenly believe that the biblical laws were meant for all people, we risk imposing a legalistic framework on a faith that was meant to be about freedom, love, and faith. The core of Christianity, as taught by Jesus, is not about adherence to laws but about loving god and loving others. The laws given to Israel were a part of a specific covenant, but that covenant has been fulfilled and transformed in Christ. Non-Jews, or Gentiles, were never meant to follow the old laws. Instead, they were invited to enter into a new relationship with god, one that transcends the old boundaries.

The historical context of biblical mythology is crucial in understanding this. The laws were written at a time when Israel was a small, distinct nation surrounded by other peoples with different beliefs and practices. The laws were a way to keep the Israelites separate, to protect their identity as god's chosen people, and to maintain the holiness of their community. These laws were never meant to be a universal moral code or a way to govern the whole world. They were specific to a particular time and people, and they were meant to preserve the integrity of that community until the coming of Christ, when the message of god's love and salvation would be available to all people, not just the Jews.

Understanding that biblical laws and traditions were never meant for non-Jewish people helps us avoid the mistake of trying to impose them on others. It also allows us to appreciate the deeper message of biblical mythology, that the relationship between god and humanity is not about following a set of rules but about faith, love, and transformation. The teachings of Jesus, and the early church, make it clear that the gospel is for all people, regardless of their background. The old laws were part of god's plan for Israel, but they were never meant to be a universal standard for all people. The message of Christ is much broader and much more inclusive, offering a new way of living that goes beyond the old laws and traditions.

What It Means To Be A Disciple Of Christ

Being a Disciple of Christ is all about following Jesus, but not just in a surface-level way. It's more than just saying you're a follower or attending church on Sundays. A disciple is someone who makes a conscious decision to model their life after Jesus, his actions, his way of thinking, and his values. It means truly living in the way he taught and making those teachings part of your day-to-day existence. It's not about being perfect. It's about making an effort to continuously learn from him and live according to the principles he set out.

In biblical mythology, discipleship isn't something you do when it's convenient, nor is it just about following rules or rituals. It's about a commitment to a relationship with Jesus. The original disciples were often ordinary people like fishermen, tax collectors, and everyday folks who left everything behind to walk with him, learn from him, and help spread his message. This wasn't easy. They didn't fully understand everything he was teaching at the time, but they trusted that his path was one worth following, even when it didn't always make sense. Their commitment wasn't to a set of doctrines but to a living, breathing relationship with Jesus.

historical context also sheds light on what being a disciple meant back then. Discipleship in the first century wasn't just about knowledge. It was about immersion. Disciples were meant to embody what they learned, not just memorize teachings. They were expected to walk with their teacher, share in their struggles, and reflect their teacher's values in every part of their lives. That's why Jesus didn't just tell his disciples about the Kingdom of god; he showed them how to live it out. He lived in a way that was radically different from the social norms of the time, challenging them to think differently about power, service, love, and justice. Discipleship meant being willing to turn away from societal expectations and follow his example, even if it was uncomfortable or went against the grain.

The whole idea of being a disciple also hinges on humility. Jesus wasn't interested in followers who were just looking to elevate themselves or gain power. Instead, he called his disciples to serve, to help others, and to show love without seeking anything in return. This isn't easy, especially in a world that often tells us to prioritize our own success and status. But the message is clear: true discipleship is about serving others, not being served. It's about loving others even when it's difficult and about putting the needs of others before our own.

Being a disciple of Christ is also about personal transformation. It's about allowing Jesus' teachings to shape you from the inside out. It's not just about acting in a certain way because it's expected or following rules to stay out of trouble. It's about letting love, humility, and service become a part of your nature. Discipleship is a journey, one that requires growth and change. You don't stay the same when you commit to following Christ; you become more like him. And that process of becoming more like him often involves wrestling with tough questions, facing challenges, and sometimes even experiencing doubt. But through it all, discipleship is about continually coming back to that relationship with Jesus, trusting in his guidance, and allowing that relationship to transform you.

In practical terms, being a disciple of Christ means trying to live according to his example in every area of life. It's about how we treat others, how we view ourselves, and how we respond to the world around us. It's about living a life of kindness, compassion, and justice, even when it feels difficult. It's about resisting the urge to conform to the pressures and temptations of the world and instead choosing the narrow path that Jesus spoke about, the path that leads to life. Discipleship doesn't promise an easy life, but it offers a fulfilling one. It's a call to radical love and service in a world that often values the opposite.

Being a disciple of Christ, then, is an ongoing process. It's a decision to follow Jesus every single day, no matter what. And it's a decision that transforms you, slowly but surely, into someone who reflects his love and grace in the world. The journey may be long and at times challenging, but it's also deeply rewarding. In the end, being a disciple of Christ is about more than just believing in him. It's about living for him, modeling your life on his example, and letting his teachings shape who you are.

A prophet of god stands apart from others because they carry a message that is not their own but comes from god. Their purpose isn't to share their own ideas or opinions but to convey divine wisdom, often about the present and future. Prophets aren't just people who predict things; they seem to act as god's spokespersons, revealing divine wisdom to the people. In biblical mythology, prophets were called to speak on god's behalf, sometimes delivering warnings of judgment, calls for repentance, or messages of hope. What makes a prophet distinct is that they aren't motivated by personal gain or the desire for power. They speak because they seem to be compelled by god, even when the message is uncomfortable or unwelcome.

One of the most distinctive features of a prophet is their deep connection to god. Prophets often spend time in prayer, fasting, or solitude, seeking to understand divine wisdom and prepare themselves to deliver the message with clarity and authority. They don't just talk about god; they experience a profound, direct relationship with the divine. This connection is often marked by visions, dreams, or an intense inner conviction that what they are saying is not of their own making. Prophets usually claim to be chosen by god, and the calling can come in unexpected ways. Moses, for example, was called from a burning bush, and Jonah was sent on a mission to Nineveh, reluctant at first but ultimately compelled by the message he was given.

historically, prophets were often outsiders. They weren't part of the established religious or political systems, and this made their role even more challenging. They spoke truth to power, challenging the status quo and calling out injustice, corruption, and idolatry. Prophets like Isaiah, Jeremiah, and Amos weren't afraid to criticize the kings, priests, and people who had turned away from god's teachings. They often faced persecution or rejection because their messages didn't align with what those in power wanted to hear. A prophet's role wasn't to gain popularity or support; it was to speak the truth, regardless of the consequences.

Another feature of a prophet is their moral integrity. Prophets are not just messengers; they are also examples of how to live according to god's will. They lead by example, often living lives that demonstrate the very principles they preach. They call the people to repentance not just with words, but with their actions. For instance, the prophet Elijah didn't just speak against the worship of false gods; he challenged the prophets of Baal to a dramatic contest on Mount Carmel to prove that the god of Israel was the one true god. A prophet's life is meant to reflect their message, showing others what it looks like to live in accordance with god's will.

Another characteristic of prophets is their ability to see beyond the present moment. They are often visionaries, able to perceive a bigger picture that others may not see. Their prophecies aren't just about what is happening in the here and now; they point toward a future that may seem distant or impossible. Prophets like Daniel and Ezekiel saw visions of kingdoms, nations, and events that would unfold long after their time. These visions weren't just predictions but invitations to reflect on the course of history and human behavior. Prophets often spoke of a future where justice would prevail, peace would reign, and god's kingdom would come to earth, but they also warned that things would get worse before they got better.

The message of a prophet is often urgent and relentless. Prophets are not just speaking for the sake of speaking; they are driven by a sense of duty to god and to the people they are sent to. Their messages are not easy to deliver, and often, they are not received well. Prophets are called to speak even when they know their words will be rejected. Jeremiah is known as the weeping prophet because of the sorrow he felt for the people who ignored his warnings. But despite the rejection, the prophet's task is to keep delivering the message, trusting that it will bear fruit in the long run, even if the people don't respond immediately.

One of the most compelling features of a prophet is their unwavering commitment to god's truth, regardless of how difficult it may be. They are not swayed by public opinion, the pressures of society, or even their own fears. They stand firm in the truth they have been given, even when it costs them everything. Prophets often endured personal suffering, rejection, and isolation. The prophet Hosea, for example, was commanded by god to marry a woman who would be unfaithful to him as a symbol of Israel's unfaithfulness to god. This personal sacrifice illustrates the depth of commitment a prophet must have to their calling.

In the end, a prophet's distinctive features are not just in the messages they deliver but in the way they live out those messages. They are deeply connected to god, committed to truth, and willing to stand against injustice, no matter the personal cost. A prophet is more than a mere spokesperson; they are a living example of the divine principles they proclaim. Their role is essential because they help people see where they have gone astray and point them back to the path of righteousness, even when that path seems hard to follow.

The role of the Apostles in the story of Christianity is deeply important because they were the ones who took Christian teachings and spread them to the world. They were not just followers; they were chosen by Jesus to be his closest companions and to continue his mission after his death. The Apostles were ordinary people, but their role was extraordinary. They were handpicked by Jesus to witness his life, learn from his teachings, and carry on his work. Their task was to not only spread the gospel but to help establish the foundation of what would become the early church.

In biblical mythology, the Apostles were often shown as people who were transformed by their relationship with Jesus. Before they met him, many of them were just fishermen or tax collectors, living lives that weren't particularly extraordinary. But once they were called, their lives were changed in dramatic ways. They left everything behind to follow him, and in doing so, they took on a responsibility that would shape the future of Christianity. The Apostles witnessed the miracles of Jesus, heard his teachings firsthand, and were with him during some of the most pivotal moments of his life, including the crucifixion and the resurrection. This personal experience gave them authority and credibility when they went out to share his message with others.

The Apostles were not just chosen to spread the word; they were also given a unique role in establishing the early church. They were the first leaders of the Christian community, and they played a crucial part in organizing and guiding the believers after Jesus' ascension. They helped to solidify the teachings of Jesus, making sure that they were passed down accurately to others. The Apostles didn't just teach; they helped to build the structures and practices that would become the foundation of Christian worship. They were responsible for ordaining new leaders, guiding the communities of believers, and making decisions that would affect the growth of the church.

historically, the Apostles played a key role in spreading Christianity beyond the Jewish community. In the beginning, Jesus' followers were mostly Jewish, and they saw the movement as a continuation of their own faith. But as the Apostles went out into the world, they began to see that the message of Jesus was not just for Jews but for all people. This shift is particularly evident in the work of the Apostle Paul, who, though not one of the original Twelve, became one of the most influential figures in spreading Christianity throughout the Roman Empire. Paul's letters, which are now part of the New Testament, were critical in explaining the message of Jesus to non-Jews and in establishing Christian teachings that would spread across the Mediterranean world.

The Apostles also had to face significant challenges. The early Christian movement was not universally accepted, and the Apostles often faced persecution for their beliefs. They were arrested, beaten, and sometimes killed for spreading the message of Jesus. The Roman Empire, in particular, viewed the movement as a threat to their authority, which meant that the Apostles had to be bold and courageous in their mission. Despite the risks, they continued to preach and teach, convinced of the truth of their message. Their perseverance in the face of adversity helped to establish Christianity as a movement that could not be easily silenced or stopped.

What is interesting is that the Apostles were not just leaders in a religious sense; they were also witnesses to the very heart of Christianity. Their role was not just about preaching; it was about embodying the teachings of Jesus in their own lives. They were called to live as Jesus did, to serve others, showing love, and spreading peace. In a way, they became living examples of what it meant to follow Christ. Their actions and decisions were a reflection of their belief in Jesus and his teachings. Through their leadership, they set the standard for how the early Christian communities were meant to live, shaping the way that followers of Jesus would continue to live in the generations that followed.

The role of the Apostles also extended to the establishment of doctrine. They were responsible for deciding which teachings were truly reflective of the message of Jesus and which ones were not. This was not an easy task, especially as the early church began to grow and new ideas started to emerge. The Apostles had to wrestle with questions about the nature of god, the relationship between Jesus and the Father, and the role of the Holy Spirit.

The Apostles also had a crucial role in maintaining unity within the early church. As the message of Jesus spread, new communities of believers were formed in different regions. The Apostles were responsible for making sure that these communities stayed true to the teachings of Jesus and maintained a sense of unity. They communicated with one another through letters, and they also sent representatives to visit different communities to encourage and strengthen the believers. This work of maintaining unity was important because it helped ensure that Christianity didn't become fragmented or divided in its early years.

Overall, the role of the Apostles was multifaceted and deeply impactful. They were the foundation upon which the Christian faith was built, and their work continues to resonate today. They were not just messengers; they were leaders, teachers, and examples of what it meant to follow Christ. Their sacrifices, their teachings, and their perseverance in the face of persecution played a critical role in the growth of Christianity. Without their commitment, Christianity might not have spread in the way it did, and the church might not have taken the shape that it has today. Their role was vital, and it was one that they took on with a sense of responsibility and devotion to the message they had received from Jesus.

The Nonbeliever And Divine Wisdom

When we talk about the nonbeliever in the context of divine wisdom, there's often a lot of confusion and tension. Many people have been taught to think of nonbelievers as somehow distant or disconnected from divine wisdom, but this is where we have to pause and think. The idea that divine wisdom is only for those who already believe is problematic, to say the least. If we really consider the broader scope of biblical mythology and what it's trying to communicate, it seems clear that divine wisdom is much bigger than just a group of believers; it's for everyone, whether they believe it or not.

First off, when you examine biblical mythology, you see that the divine message has always been one of inclusion, even for those who might not be a believer. If you go back to the Old Testament, there's an understanding that god's work extends beyond just Israel. Even in the laws and stories meant for the Israelites, there's often a call to care for the foreigner, the stranger, and the outsider. This isn't just a minor detail; it's a recurring theme. And in the New Testament, Jesus' teachings are radical in the sense that he regularly reached out to those on the fringes of society, those who weren't necessarily part of the Jewish faith. He dined with sinners, healed the sick, and showed kindness to outsiders. This wasn't just a theological exercise; it was an active engagement with people who, at the time, weren't seen as part of god's chosen people. And this wasn't just about trying to convert them, it was about demonstrating the pinciples of love and grace in a way that was tangible, immediate, and accessible to everyone.

In fact, some of the best examples of people understanding divine wisdom in a way that bypasses traditional belief come from nonbelievers themselves. Take the story of the centurion in the gospels, for example. Here's a Roman soldier, a man who isn't part of the Jewish faith, yet he's the one who recognizes Jesus' authority and expresses faith in a way that astounds Jesus. This isn't an isolated incident.

Throughout biblical mythology, there's a sense that divine wisdom isn't limited by whether or not someone subscribes to a certain belief system. The recognition of divine power, truth, and goodness can come from all corners of society, from people who wouldn't typically be seen as part of the religious establishment.

When we focus solely on the idea that divine wisdom is only for believers, we risk missing the larger point: divine wisdom is meant to reach and transform the hearts of all people. The gospel, when it's fully understood, isn't just a set of beliefs; it's an invitation to life, justice, peace, and the flourishing of humanity. It's about seeing the image of the divine in others, regardless of whether they believe the same things we do. If you look at the writings in the New Testament, especially in the letters of Paul, you see a strong emphasis on the idea that faith isn't about following a particular set of rules but about living in a way that reflects god's character, loving others, seeking justice, and working for peace. This message has always been broader than just a narrow religious group.

What makes divine wisdom so powerful is its ability to transcend human divisions. The moment we start thinking that divine wisdom is only for those who believe as we do, we've already misunderstood the essence of the gospel. God isn't in the business of drawing lines between people based on belief alone. The message is for anyone who is open to it, whether they're aware of it or not, or whether they identify with a particular faith or not. The focus should never solely be on conversion or doctrinal agreement; it's about inviting people into a relationship with the divine that's about love, justice, and the pursuit of a better world.

For nonbelievers, divine wisdom is still relevant and present. It's in the beauty of creation, the wonder of human connection, the fight for justice, and the desire for peace. These are all expressions of the divine that can be understood and experienced outside of the framework of religious belief. Divine wisdom isn't just something that exists within the confines of scripture or church, it's something that is embedded in the very fabric of life, in the everyday moments of kindness, the struggles for truth, and the desire for a world that reflects goodness. Nonbelievers can see and feel this, even if they don't frame it in religious terms.

It's also important to acknowledge that not everyone who finds divine wisdom in this broader sense will necessarily recognize it as such, and that's okay. There's no pressure to label it. Just because someone doesn't identify as a believer doesn't mean they are not engaging with or responding to the divine in their own way. In fact, some of the most profound expressions of love, compassion, and justice have come from people who don't hold to traditional religious beliefs. Their actions can be just as much a reflection of divine wisdom as anything we might find in a sermon or scripture. The divine doesn't just work within the bounds of religious belief, it works within the heart of humanity itself, calling us to be better, to love more deeply, and to seek justice.

Divine wisdom, then, is not just for believers; it's for the world. It's not about making people adhere to a specific belief system; it's about inviting them into a deeper understanding of love, grace, and the divine reality that transcends human limitations. The nonbeliever, in their search for meaning, justice, and goodness, is already engaging with divine wisdom in a way that reflects the truth that the divine is with us all. Whether or not they consciously recognize it, they are not outside the reach of the divine message. And maybe that's the beauty of it: divine wisdom is a whisper in the wind, an invitation for all to hear, regardless of where they are in their journey.

The Nonbeliever And The Divine

Nonbelievers often approach questions about human existence, morality, and meaning through a lens of reason and logic. This perspective doesn't inherently lack depth or significance; in fact, it often offers a rich and thoughtful way of navigating the complexities of life. Without a personal relationship with the divine, nonbelievers naturally turn to other tools to understand the world. For many, science becomes a primary means of uncovering the mysteries of the universe. Through observation, experimentation, and analysis, science offers explanations that can be tested, repeated, and refined over time. The scientific method doesn't just provide answers, it also encourages questions, making it an ever-evolving process of discovery.

Critical thinking, too, plays a crucial role in the nonbeliever's quest for understanding. Instead of relying on traditions or doctrines that may seem unprovable or intangible, nonbelievers are more likely to scrutinize beliefs, questioning their foundation and examining their implications. In this way, the nonbeliever's approach to life can be seen as a search for truth that's grounded in evidence, logic, and a commitment to understanding the world as it is, rather than how it might be imagined. There's a certain discipline involved in taking a step back and evaluating one's assumptions, not accepting things at face value, and engaging with different perspectives to form a more complete picture.

For nonbelievers, moral questions are often examined through the lens of human experience, societal well-being, and the consequences of actions. Without a divine lawgiver to provide clear commandments, nonbelievers tend to base their understanding of right and wrong on human relationships and the practical outcomes of behaviors. Ethics becomes a matter of how actions affect others and how societies can function more harmoniously. Concepts like justice, empathy, and fairness are frequently emphasized, with the understanding that these values are important for the collective good, even if they don't stem from a religious authority. There's an underlying assumption that humans can reason through moral questions and come to conclusions that benefit everyone, not just those who share a particular faith.

Meaning in life, for nonbelievers, is often derived from personal experience, relationships, and contributions to society. Without a belief in an afterlife or a divine purpose, nonbelievers find significance in the here and now. They may seek to make the world a better place through their work, their actions, and their relationships with others. The idea of leaving a legacy, of creating something lasting, is often central to their understanding of purpose. Instead of waiting for meaning to be handed down from a higher power, nonbelievers take the responsibility upon themselves to find or create meaning in their daily lives.

One of the advantages of this perspective is that it allows for flexibility and adaptation. Since the nonbeliever doesn't rely on rigid, unchanging doctrines, they can change their views as new information arises. This openness to change doesn't mean a lack of conviction but rather a commitment to refining one's understanding of the world based on the best available evidence. It's a recognition that knowledge is incomplete and that our understanding of truth should evolve as we grow and learn more about ourselves and the world.

This reliance on reason and logic doesn't mean nonbelievers are necessarily cold or unfeeling. In fact, many approach questions of morality and meaning with deep empathy and compassion. They are driven by a genuine concern for the well-being of others, motivated by a sense of shared humanity rather than divine command. The nonbeliever's moral compass can still be strong, often rooted in a deep sense of justice and the desire to alleviate suffering in the world.

Nonbelievers also engage with questions of existence in ways that focus on human agency and the natural world. Since there's no belief in a higher being shaping destiny, they often focus on what humans can do to create positive change, understanding that individuals have the power to shape their futures. This emphasis on human responsibility leads to a worldview that values reason, evidence, and action in ways that can be very practical and impactful. When it comes to understanding the nature of the universe, nonbelievers look to science to provide answers that are grounded in observation and empirical data. The study of the cosmos, the evolution of life, and the workings of the human brain are all areas where reason and logic have led to profound insights about the nature of reality.

One of the challenges for nonbelievers, however, is grappling with the limitations of human understanding. While science can offer incredible insights into how things work, it doesn't always provide the answers to the deeper existential questions, like why we're here or what the ultimate purpose of life is. This is where some nonbelievers may turn to philosophy, art, or personal reflection to fill in the gaps. They might explore concepts like existentialism or humanism, which focus on individual freedom and the creation of personal meaning in a world that doesn't necessarily offer a clear, predefined purpose.

For some nonbelievers, the absence of a higher power or divine purpose doesn't diminish the richness of life. Instead, it can enhance it by encouraging a sense of personal responsibility and freedom. Without the constraints of religious dogma, they can embrace the idea that life is what we make of it, and the meaning we find in it comes from the relationships we build, the experiences we have, and the contributions we make to the world. This kind of meaning-making is often seen as more authentic because it comes from within rather than being imposed externally.

While nonbelievers may not share the same spiritual framework as believers, their approach to life is not necessarily less valuable or less meaningful. In fact, many nonbelievers find a deep sense of purpose in the natural world, human relationships, and the pursuit of knowledge. They may not look to divine revelation for guidance, but they still engage with the big questions of existence, morality, and meaning with seriousness and depth. Their search for truth and understanding, grounded in reason and logic, is a legitimate way of navigating the complexities of life, and it offers a different but equally important perspective on the human experience.

Dialogue Between Believers And Nonbelievers

Understanding and dialogue between believers and nonbelievers have never been more crucial, especially in a world that seems more divided than ever. We live in a time where people often hold strong opinions and have rigid beliefs about everything, from politics to religion, and it's easy to see the divisions growing wider. But it's precisely in this environment that we need more open conversations. When people from different backgrounds and belief systems engage with one another, they have the chance to build bridges instead of walls. For believers, it's an opportunity to share their faith in a way that respects others and invites curiosity rather than judgment. For nonbelievers, it's a chance to better understand the role that faith plays in many people's lives, and perhaps, gain a deeper understanding of the motivations behind certain beliefs.

It's easy to feel frustrated or misunderstood, especially when someone challenges your views or doesn't seem to understand where you're coming from. But it's important to recognize that every person's perspective is shaped by their own experiences, knowledge, and context. A nonbeliever may not share the same understanding of divine presence, moral guidance, or the significance of religious texts, just as a believer might struggle to grasp the logic behind rejecting faith. Neither side is inherently wrong for holding their beliefs. The key is finding a way to communicate these beliefs in a way that promotes understanding rather than deepening division.

A big part of fostering understanding comes from recognizing that dialogue is not a competition. It's not about trying to "win" the conversation by proving someone else wrong. It's about listening, asking questions, and being willing to be vulnerable enough to learn something new. A believer can share their experiences of faith, how they find comfort and direction in their belief in god, while a nonbeliever can share their views on the role of reason, science, and skepticism in their lives. Through these conversations, both sides can see the humanity in one another and recognize the shared desire for meaning, purpose, and truth, even if they approach those things in different ways.

The challenge for believers, though, is not to assume that nonbelievers are simply misguided or in need of saving. It's easy to view someone who doesn't share your beliefs as being lost or lacking in some way. But this assumption can close the door to meaningful dialogue. Instead of approaching conversations with a desire to "convert" or "fix" someone, believers should approach nonbelievers with respect and a willingness to listen. By doing so, they may gain insight into how nonbelievers find meaning in their lives and may even find common ground where they least expect it. And for nonbelievers, it's equally important to be open to the idea that someone's faith might be a deeply personal, transformative experience that can't simply be written off or dismissed. Faith for many is a source of comfort, guidance, and moral foundation. Understanding this can make the dialogue much more empathetic.

It's also worth acknowledging that not every conversation will be easy, and not everyone will be willing to engage respectfully. But it's important to not let these negative experiences sour our willingness to have these conversations. It's through persistence and patience that understanding grows. If we allow ourselves to get discouraged or shut down by one bad experience, we risk missing the opportunity for real growth and connection in future conversations.

Promoting empathy and compassion is not just about having the right words. It's about the willingness to see things from another's perspective. A believer who engages with a nonbeliever should strive to understand why they question the existence of god or reject certain teachings. What experiences have shaped their views? What are their concerns or fears? At the same time, a nonbeliever who speaks with a believer should ask what role faith plays in their life, why they find it meaningful, and what aspects of their belief give them a sense of peace and purpose. By genuinely seeking to understand one another, both sides can avoid jumping to conclusions or making judgments that can hinder meaningful dialogue.

There's also something powerful in realizing that we don't always have to agree to find common ground. Just because two people don't see eye to eye on matters of faith or philosophy doesn't mean they can't respect one another's views and work toward mutual understanding. It's possible to have deep and thoughtful discussions about religion, morality, and existence without resorting to conflict or judgment. In fact, such discussions can open up new ways of thinking and encourage growth in both parties.

In a polarized world, finding common ground requires patience, humility, and a willingness to engage in uncomfortable conversations. It's not always easy to have these conversations, especially when emotions run high or when we feel like our beliefs are being challenged. But in the end, these discussions are an opportunity to promote greater empathy and understanding. They give us the chance to learn more about each other and find ways to live in harmony despite our differences. Through these conversations, we can break down the walls of misunderstanding and build bridges that connect us in our shared humanity.

God Is Not Punishing Nonbelievers

The idea that god is punishing nonbelievers is a deeply ingrained concept in some circles, but when we really think about it, it doesn't line up with the nature of god as described in biblical mythology. God's message throughout the scriptures, if we really pay attention to the overarching themes, seems to focus more on offering love, guidance, and grace rather than on punishment. It's easy to read certain passages and think that god is out to get those who don't believe, but when we take a step back and examine things with a broader perspective, the story becomes more about god's desire to bring everyone closer rather than push people away.

It's important to consider the context of those moments in scripture that speak of judgment or punishment. Often, these ideas are tied to behaviors that go against the foundational principles of love, compassion, and justice. Biblical mythology doesn't just give a blanket statement about punishing those who don't believe; instead, it focuses more on actions that harm others or ourselves. If we take a closer look at biblical mythology, it becomes clear that what god seems to be interested in isn't punishing people for their lack of belief, but rather guiding them toward a more loving, fulfilling way of living. Nonbelievers are not being singled out for punishment just because they don't hold the same beliefs. What's more significant in the biblical message is how people treat one another and the world around them. The focus is on how individuals relate to each other, to god, and to creation.

When you look at the life and teachings of Jesus, it's impossible to miss how nonpunitive his message was. He didn't go around condemning people for not following him or for questioning god's will. Instead, he seemed to emphasize mercy, forgiveness, and understanding. He showed compassion to those who were rejected by society, including nonbelievers, and often challenged the established norms of his time. His teachings pointed to the idea that god's love is unconditional and available to all people, regardless of their level of belief. If god was truly interested in punishing nonbelievers, then Jesus' actions and messages would have been quite different. But what Jesus did was to open up the possibility of relationship with god to everyone, showing that belief wasn't a requirement for receiving god's love.

It's also essential to recognize that in biblical mythology, god's relationship with humanity has always been one of patience and long-suffering. The story of the Israelites, for example, is filled with instances of them turning away from god, yet god didn't abandon them. Even when they strayed, god provided a path for them to return, through prophets, guidance, and eventually through Jesus. This ongoing call to return to god, even after turning away, reflects a loving and patient god who doesn't punish out of anger, but rather seeks reconciliation and connection.

Another thing to consider is that the idea of god punishing nonbelievers creates an artificial divide between believers and nonbelievers. It suggests that those who don't share the same faith are somehow less deserving of love, grace, or understanding. But the reality is that people of all faiths, or no faith at all, can demonstrate love, kindness, and generosity. To label nonbelievers as deserving of punishment because of their lack of belief misses the point of what the message of god is about. The idea of punishment often reflects a human desire for justice that is rooted in misunderstanding, fear, or even pride, not the kind of justice that aligns with the deeper, more profound aspects of love and mercy in biblical mythology.

It's also worth noting that biblical mythology speaks of god's desire for all to come to knowledge and truth, but never in a way that seems punitive. The idea that nonbelievers are being punished for not believing takes the focus off the fundamental Christian message, that god's love is there for everyone, and everyone has the potential to embrace it. In fact, biblical mythology suggests that god's desire is to draw people to him, not to push them away with fear of punishment. The ultimate goal isn't for people to be scared into belief but for them to come to an understanding of the divine message, a message of love, mercy, and forgiveness.

When we view nonbelievers through a lens of understanding and empathy rather than judgment, we begin to see that the divine has no valid reason to punish them for their lack of faith. Instead, they are simply walking a different path, just as many believers are on their own unique journey. The idea that nonbelievers need to be punished ignores the fact that belief, or lack thereof, is often influenced by a person's experiences, upbringing, and circumstances, all of which are out of their control. Love and grace are not contingent upon one's ability to believe in a specific way. To suggest otherwise is to misunderstand the very nature of humanity's relationship with the divine.

In the end, the focus shouldn't be on punishment, but on love. God's message is one of love and hope, not fear. It's about finding a way to live with purpose, to connect with others in a meaningful way, and to seek out the kind of truth that leads to peace. Nonbelievers are not being punished for not believing; they are simply on a different path, one that is just as valid as any other. The task for believers is not to condemn those who don't share their faith but to live in a way that exemplifies the love, mercy, and grace that are at the heart of god's message.

Eidotheosophy For Nonbelievers

It might seem a bit odd to consider that atheists could find any value in something rooted in biblical mythology, but when I think about it, I realize there's no reason why they couldn't use the framework of eidotheosophy to bridge the gap between faith and reason. Eidotheosophy is really about finding a clear distinction between divine wisdom (or universal understanding) and human interests, and that's something that can resonate beyond the boundaries of religious belief. While atheists don't have a theological doctrine to draw universal understanding from, they have something just as powerful: philosophy. Philosophy, especially in its most thoughtful and honest forms, offers a rich well of ideas that have been tested, questioned, and refined over centuries. Those ideas are not bound by specific doctrines or sacred texts but by a shared human quest for understanding.

For an atheist, this could be incredibly useful. They may not turn to biblical mythology or any other religious texts as a source of authority, but they still seek the same kind of clarity and wisdom that those texts aim to offer. The beauty of philosophy is that it's not tied to any one tradition. It doesn't require you to accept a particular set of beliefs to start engaging with it. So, when applying eidotheosophy, an atheist could still use the same methodology of separating universal understanding from human biases and interests, but instead of looking at biblical mythology for guidance, they might turn to the works of Plato, Aristotle, Kant, or any number of other thinkers. What's important is not the source of the wisdom, but the process of refining that wisdom to understand the world more clearly.

Eidotheosophy is about applying reason, logic, and research to extract universal truths while discarding the human interests that often distort them. The concept of divine wisdom, for those who don't hold religious beliefs, could be replaced with the idea of objective truth or universal understanding. This allows them to adopt the core philosophy of eidotheosophy without needing to adhere to religious doctrines. They can separate what is truly beneficial or ethical from the noise of personal biases, societal pressures, or cultural expectations. This isn't about rejecting the validity of religious wisdom; it's about using the same critical approach to all sources of knowledge, whether religious or secular.

But the real question here is: what value would this have for an atheist? Honestly, that's something only they could answer. I can't speak for them. But I do think the appeal of a rational, reasoned approach to understanding the world is universal. Atheists, like anyone else, are looking for answers to the big questions. What's the purpose of life? What's the right thing to do in a given situation? How can we live ethically in a complex, often unjust world? These are questions that don't require a belief in a divine being to answer, but they do require thoughtful reflection and careful analysis. And this is exactly what eidotheosophy provides: a framework to approach these questions in a thoughtful, reasoned way while avoiding the pitfalls of human interests or biases that often cloud judgment.

The great thing about eidotheosophy is that it doesn't impose any particular belief on anyone. It doesn't require an atheist to believe in god or accept any religious doctrine. It simply encourages critical thinking, a willingness to question, and an openness to wisdom that transcends the human tendency to let personal agendas distort truth. In a way, this can be a refreshing perspective for anyone, atheist or otherwise, who is tired of the dogma and limitations often found in more rigid belief systems. It offers a way to explore ethical principles and universal truths without feeling confined by tradition or authority.

Of course, how an atheist might use this philosophy is up to them. It could provide a way to engage with the deeper questions of existence without needing to resort to religious explanations or embrace a particular belief system. They could find in it a tool for separating the moral and ethical wisdom from any biases, allowing for a clearer, more objective understanding of the world. Alternatively, they might simply appreciate the fact that eidotheosophy offers a space where reason and wisdom are valued above all else, without the need for spiritual hierarchy or divine authority. The flexibility of the approach is one of its most appealing qualities. It can fit into a variety of worldviews, not because it compromises on its principles, but because it leaves room for individuals to find their own truths.

Ultimately, whether an atheist finds value in eidotheosophy is a deeply personal matter. It's not about trying to convince them to adopt a religious belief or adopt the principles of biblical mythology. It's about offering a framework that encourages open-mindedness, critical thinking, and the search for wisdom in all its forms. For some atheists, this might be a helpful way to navigate the complexities of life, while for others, it might not resonate at all. Either way, the idea that eidotheosophy can serve as a bridge between faith and reason is something that should be explored, not dismissed. The beauty of this philosophy is that it doesn't require anyone to change their core beliefs; it simply provides another lens through which to understand the world more clearly.

Love, The Divine Message

At its core, the message of biblical mythology is rooted in love. When you examine biblical mythology, it's clear that love isn't just an isolated idea but the very foundation of divine wisdom. The most important commandment in biblical mythology is to love god with all your heart, soul, mind, and strength, but equally important is the call to love your neighbor as yourself. These are not just abstract principles; they are the heart of the divine message. Love is not something god does occasionally or something that is merely a nice idea. Love is who god is, and it is through this lens that biblical mythology is meant to be understood.

When we move to the life and teachings of Jesus, this message of love becomes even clearer. Jesus didn't just talk about love; he embodied it in everything he did. He taught us to forgive, not just once or twice, but seventy-seven times, which is to say, endlessly. Forgiveness, in this sense, isn't about excusing wrongdoings but about releasing the hold that anger and bitterness have over our lives. Jesus' teachings about love also focus on loving our enemies, a concept that seems radical in many ways, especially considering the world we live in. Jesus didn't say we should only love those who love us back or those who are easy to love. He said that we should love even those who oppose us, those who hurt us, and those who do not return our love. This, in itself, is a radical call to transcend the natural human instinct for revenge or retribution and to instead offer compassion, kindness, and understanding.

Jesus also taught us to care for the poor and oppressed. In many ways, biblical mythology presents a god who consistently sides with the marginalized, the vulnerable, and those who are suffering. Whether it's the widow, the orphan, or the poor, biblical teachings continually urge us to extend our love in tangible ways to those who are struggling. Jesus told parables about helping those in need, like the Good Samaritan, who, despite being an outsider, went out of his way to help someone who was hurting. Love in this context isn't just an emotional feeling but an active choice to care for others, to take action on behalf of those who might otherwise be overlooked or ignored. Jesus consistently preached that true love isn't measured by how much we have or how comfortable our lives are, but by how much we are willing to give, especially when it means helping those who can't repay us.

The divine message also includes a call for peace and justice. Jesus said, "Blessed are the peacemakers, for they will be called children of god." This idea of peace is not just the absence of conflict, but a deeper kind of peace that comes from justice being done, from people living in right relationship with each other, and from the reconciliation of brokenness. Justice, in biblical terms, is not about punishment or retribution but about setting things right, restoring balance, and ensuring that every person is treated with dignity and fairness. The call to love, therefore, isn't passive. It's not about simply feeling good thoughts toward others. It's about actively working to make the world a better, more just, and more peaceful place for everyone.

Jesus' call to love is not just about grand gestures or lofty ideals, but about the small, everyday choices we make. It's in the way we treat others, especially those who are most difficult to love. It's in how we approach our communities, how we engage with those in need, and how we work for peace and justice in the world. Love in the divine sense isn't something that can be confined to a specific group of people or a set of actions; it's something that encompasses all of humanity. The divine message is not just a moral teaching or a religious principle. It is a way of life that calls us to be fully human, to act with compassion, fairness, and peace, and to recognize that every person we encounter is deserving of our love and respect.

Understanding God's Nature

When we look at biblical mythology, we see that god is not a one-dimensional figure. God's nature is multifaceted, and biblical mythology presents a picture of god that is rich in complexity. If we try to grasp god's true essence, it's essential to focus on three key aspects: love and compassion, justice and fairness, and god's relationship with humanity. These are not isolated concepts, but interwoven elements that form the foundation of how we understand god's actions and intentions in the world.

Love and compassion are perhaps the most emphasized qualities in biblical mythology. Time and again, we see god depicted as someone who deeply cares for creation, particularly for humanity. From the very beginning, the creation story suggests a god who takes great care in shaping the world and creating human beings in a way that reflects a unique relationship between god and humanity. It's through this lens of love that we understand god's interactions with the world. God's love is not limited or conditional, but it's described as enduring, unconditional, and reaching out to all people, regardless of their faults or failures. When we consider the life of Jesus, we see an embodiment of this love. Jesus wasn't about judgment or punishment but about healing, helping, and showing compassion for those who were hurting or marginalized. Jesus' actions and teachings consistently point to a loving god who doesn't turn away from people in their brokenness but instead draws close to them, offering mercy and hope.

Justice and fairness are also deeply embedded in the biblical depiction of god. While love and compassion often take the spotlight, god's commitment to justice is equally important. Biblical mythology frequently addresses the issue of justice, often focusing on god's concern for the vulnerable and oppressed. The prophets, in particular, speak about god's desire for a just society where the poor are cared for, the widow is not abandoned, and the oppressed are freed. In the Psalms, for example, god is described as a defender of the weak, one who upholds the cause of the righteous and punishes those who harm others. But this justice is not vengeful or petty. It's not about retribution for its own sake, but about setting things right. It's a justice that seeks to restore balance and ensure that all people have a fair opportunity to live in peace and dignity. This aspect of god's nature speaks to a commitment to the well-being of all people, especially those who might otherwise be overlooked or taken advantage of.

god's relationship with humanity is perhaps the most central theme in biblical mythology. Biblical mythology presents a picture of a god who desires a relationship with humanity, a relationship marked by love, but also by respect and freedom. The relationship is not one of coercion or manipulation but one in which human beings are given the choice to respond to god's love. From the Garden of Eden to the covenant with Israel, biblical mythology tells a story of god reaching out to people, inviting them into a deeper connection with god's divine purpose. But this relationship is not always easy or straightforward. Biblical mythology shows that humanity, time and again, strays from god's guidance, yet god does not abandon them. Instead, god continues to call people back, offering grace and a path to reconciliation. This relational aspect of god's nature speaks to a deep, patient love that is always open to those willing to return, no matter how far they have wandered.

These three aspects, love and compassion, justice and fairness, and god's relationship with humanity, are foundational to understanding god in the biblical narrative. They are not separate or contradictory qualities, but rather intertwined elements of a divine nature that seeks to engage with the world in a meaningful way. The love that god offers is not just an emotional feeling, but an active force that works through justice and mercy. Justice, in turn, is not cold and punitive but rooted in the desire to see the world made right. And through it all, god remains steadfast in wanting a relationship with humanity, one that is based on mutual respect and a willingness to seek understanding.

To truly understand god, we have to see these attributes not as abstract concepts but as deeply practical realities that shape the way god influences the world. They are the lens through which we can interpret everything that happens in the biblical story, from the life of Jesus to the promises made to Israel and beyond. Understanding these elements of god's nature helps us to see how they can inform our own relationships with others, our pursuit of justice, and our engagement with the world. It also helps us make sense of the more challenging parts of biblical mythology, where god's actions may seem harsh or difficult to understand. When we remember that all of god's message is grounded in love, justice, and a desire for relationship, we can approach these concepts with a deeper sense of understanding and empathy.

In biblical mythology, the Law, as given to the Israelites, was an essential structure for their society and spiritual life. It provided a clear framework for ethical behaviour, setting boundaries and guiding individuals on how to live justly and in harmony with god's will. But as much as the Law served a purpose in regulating conduct, it had its limitations. It functioned primarily as a set of rules for external behaviour rather than addressing the deeper, internal issues that contribute to suffering. While the commandments outlined what was right and wrong, they did not dig into the root causes of why people acted unethically in the first place. The Law's focus was on actions, whether you followed the rules or not, but it didn't offer a path to address the motivations, desires, or emotions that drive unethical behaviour.

The Law was never designed to bring about spiritual transformation. It told people what to do, but it didn't transform their hearts or change their inner nature. It couldn't cleanse the mind of destructive thoughts or heal the soul of deep-seated pain. The system of sacrifices and offerings provided some form of atonement for unethical behaviour, but these were often repeated without changing the individual on a fundamental level. The Law's repetitive nature served as a reminder of the concept of sin and its consequences, but it didn't offer a lasting cure for the pain and suffering that humanity grapples with. It pointed to the need for something deeper, something that could touch the very core of human existence. It didn't provide a way to overcome the unethical tendencies embedded in human nature.

In this sense, the Law acted more as a mirror, reflecting humanity's shortcomings. It made it clear that people were incapable of acting ethically without guidance. This realization of the Law's limitations is a crucial moment in biblical mythology. It sets the stage for the need for a deeper intervention, a solution that goes beyond just rules and regulations. The Law made it clear that, while it provided a ethical framework, it wasn't enough to bring about the transformation necessary for true reconciliation with the divine. The Law, by its nature, exposed humanity's inability to live up to the divine standard. It showed the need for something greater, something that would not just regulate external behaviour but offer a new way of living, rooted in love, compassion, and spiritual renewal.

The story of biblical mythology moves from the Law to a deeper revelation of god's plan. While the Law was important in its time and had a role to play in shaping the moral landscape, it wasn't the final answer. It appears that it always meant to point beyond itself. The Law was like a placeholder, a preparation for something that would offer true healing, transformation, and spiritual guidance. This is where the teachings of Jesus and the concept of grace come into play. Jesus came to fulfill the Law, not by abolishing it, but by offering a way to move beyond its limitations. He showed that what was truly needed wasn't just outward obedience but a heart transformation. Through love, forgiveness, and the power of grace, Jesus provided the means to overcome the power of sin and death.

The limitations of the Law are an essential part of understanding the broader narrative of biblical mythology. The Law revealed the need for a deeper spiritual solution, one that would address the causes of pain and suffering. It made it clear that humanity needed more than rules; it needed transformation from the inside out. The Law's inability to provide a path to spiritual reformation set the stage for the arrival of a teacher who would offer a new way of life that would lead to true healing, reconciliation, and spiritual freedom.

Love Is A Commitment

The divine message of love is one of the simplest yet most profound ideas found in biblical mythology. It distills the complexity of religious life into two interconnected commands, urging us to direct our hearts toward the divine and extend that love outward to the people around us. At its core, this message invites us to see love not as a passive feeling but as an active commitment. Loving god means more than worship and rituals; it means aligning our values with compassion, justice, and mercy. Loving our neighbour challenges us to break out of selfishness and recognize the shared humanity that binds us all.

While this message is straightforward, human history shows how often it has been misunderstood or ignored. Believers have claimed to follow god's teachings while engaging in acts of discrimination, exclusion, and even violence. Whether it was through religious wars, systems of oppression justified by scripture, or the marginalization of vulnerable communities, many have fallen short of living out this call to love. These failures reveal the tension between the ideals of faith and the realities of human behaviour. They remind us how easily divine teachings can be distorted when self-interest or prejudice takes precedence over compassion and humility.

The command to love one's neighbour is deeply tied to social justice. It goes beyond personal morality and enters the realm of collective responsibility. If we truly love our neighbours, we must care about the systems and structures that affect their lives. This means addressing issues like poverty, inequality, and injustice. It means recognizing that love isn't just a private virtue but a public ethic. The prophets in biblical mythology constantly reminded Israel of this, calling out those who exploited the poor and neglected the vulnerable while claiming to honour god. They understood that faith without justice is empty, that worship without care for others is hollow.

Living out this message also requires acknowledging our interconnectedness. No one exists in isolation. Our choices, big and small, ripple outward and affect others in ways we may not even realize. Whether it's the way we treat the people we encounter daily or the larger societal decisions we support, our actions matter. Loving our neighbour means taking responsibility for how our lives intersect with theirs. It challenges us to think about the impact of our privilege, the fairness of our systems, and the ways we can use our influence to uplift others rather than harm them.

The call to love is also a call to build communities that reflect those values. It's not enough for individuals to act with love; societies need to embody it too. That means creating spaces where everyone is treated with dignity, where differences are respected, and where the needs of the marginalized are met. It's about fostering environments where people feel seen, valued, and supported. This vision isn't a utopian ideal, it's a practical concept. It starts with small, intentional acts and grows into a collective movement toward justice and compassion.

At the heart of this divine message is a challenge. It asks us to go beyond comfort and convenience, to love when it's difficult, and to see others not as strangers or enemies but as part of the same human family. It calls us to reflect love in our actions, even when it costs us something. It's not an easy path, but it's one that offers the potential for profound transformation, both personally and collectively. By striving to live out this message, we can work toward a world where love is not just an ideal but a reality woven into the fabric of our communities.

The Divine Plan

The idea of a divine plan is both grand and deeply personal. In biblical mythology, this concept speaks to the intricate balance between a universal design and individual purpose. It suggests that the divine, in infinite wisdom, has crafted a unique path for each of us, a plan that aligns with the broader intentions for creation while honouring the singularity of every soul. This belief can be both comforting and challenging, offering a sense of purpose while calling us to a level of accountability and trust that doesn't always come naturally.

Divine plans are not handed to us in neatly wrapped packages. They often require discovery, discernment, and patience. We may start with a vague sense of direction or a deep longing for something greater, but understanding that purpose can take time. It involves listening, reflecting, and sometimes struggling with the uncertainties of life. Even in biblical mythology, we see figures like Abraham, Moses, and Jonah wrestling with their divine callings. Their journeys remind us that discovering our purpose is rarely straightforward. It's more like a winding road, with detours and unexpected turns that ultimately shape us in ways we couldn't have predicted.

Fulfilling a divine purpose is rarely easy or comfortable. It often involves leaving behind the familiar and stepping into the unknown. In biblical mythology, Moses had to confront Pharaoh, risking everything to free his people. Esther had to risk her life to save her people from annihilation. Jesus himself embraced a path of suffering and sacrifice, knowing it was central to the divine plan. These stories remind us that purpose often requires courage and perseverance. It may mean standing up for what is right when it would be easier to stay silent, or choosing a path of service when it might be more tempting to prioritize personal gain.

Challenges are an inevitable part of pursuing a divine plan. These challenges aren't necessarily signs that we are on the wrong path. They can be opportunities for growth, testing our faith, resilience, and commitment. The struggles we face can shape us, teaching us lessons that are essential to fulfilling our purpose. The Apostle Paul spoke often of his trials, describing them as tools through which his faith was refined. Challenges can also deepen our reliance on divine wisdom, reminding us that we don't have to navigate life's complexities on our own.

The idea that every individual has a divine purpose underscores the value and potential of each life. It's a reminder that we are not random or insignificant but part of something far greater than ourselves. At the same time, it calls us to take our choices seriously. If there is a plan for each of us, then how we live matters. The decisions we make, the relationships we nurture, the causes we support, and the ways we use our time and talents all become part of how we fulfill that plan.

One of the most beautiful aspects of this belief is how it encourages us to see others. If each person carries a unique purpose, it challenges us to respect and honor the journey of others, even when it looks different from our own. It reminds us that diversity in experiences, perspectives, and paths is not just a fact of life but a reflection of divine creativity. By supporting one another, we contribute to a world where everyone has the space to discover and fulfill their calling.

Living out a divine purpose doesn't mean every moment will feel significant or monumental. Sometimes it's in the quiet, everyday acts of kindness, integrity, and service where we fulfill our purpose most profoundly. The divine plan often unfolds in ordinary moments, as we choose to live with intention and align our actions with love, compassion, and truth. These small steps, taken faithfully, add up to a life of meaning and fulfillment. They remind us that while the divine plan is vast and beyond our comprehension, it is also deeply intimate, present in every choice and moment of our lives.

The call to love and serve society is at the heart of what it means to live as a believer. In biblical mythology, this message is woven throughout the teachings of prophets, apostles, and especially Jesus. Loving others is not just an abstract feeling; it is an active choice to prioritize their well-being. Service is how this love takes shape in the real world. Feeding the hungry, clothing the poor, and visiting the sick are some of the most basic examples, but the possibilities are endless. Every act of kindness, whether grand or small, is a reflection of this calling.

Standing up for justice is another essential part of this life. The mythology of biblical mythology is filled with stories of individuals and communities confronting injustice. From Moses demanding freedom for the enslaved Israelites to the prophets condemning the exploitation of the poor, the message is clear: faith and justice are deeply intertwined. Justice is not about revenge or punishment; it is about restoring balance and ensuring that all people are treated with dignity and fairness. It requires us to speak out against systems of oppression, even when doing so is uncomfortable or costly.

Being agents of change ties these elements together. It calls us to be more than passive observers in a broken world. Change requires action, and believers are tasked with leading the way. This might mean challenging outdated norms, creating inclusive spaces, or advocating for policies that uplift marginalized communities. It could involve personal transformation, working to rid ourselves of prejudices or habits that harm others. Change is not always immediate, but the commitment to making things better is what defines this part of the call.

Loving and serving others, standing up for justice, and being agents of change require courage and humility. These are not easy tasks, and they often involve sacrifice. Serving others can be exhausting, especially when it feels unreciprocated. Fighting for justice can be disheartening, particularly in the face of opposition or slow progress. Creating change can be overwhelming, especially when the problems seem too big to tackle. But these are not solitary efforts. Believers are part of a larger community and draw strength from the divine to persevere.

These callings are not optional add-ons to faith. They are central to what it means to live in alignment with divine wisdom. They challenge us to live beyond ourselves, to recognize that our lives are connected to those of others. Serving others and pursuing justice are how we reflect divine love in the world. Change is how we make that love visible in new and powerful ways. Together, they form a life that is not just meaningful but transformative, both for ourselves and for the world around us.

The idea of heaven often gets boxed into a vision of the afterlife, a distant realm we hope to reach someday. This perspective can make it feel abstract or irrelevant to the struggles and joys of everyday life. But when we dig into the heart of biblical mythology, it becomes clear that heaven isn't just a future destination. It is a present possibility, something that can be realized here and now when we align our lives with divine wisdom. Utopia, in this sense, is not about escapism or waiting for a better world to arrive. It's about actively creating that better world in the spaces we inhabit today.

Bringing heaven to earth begins with embodying the values that characterize divine wisdom, which are compassion, justice, love, and humility. When we approach our relationships and communities with these principles, we start to see glimpses of a utopian society. Imagine a world where people prioritize the well-being of others, where justice is not an ideal but a lived reality, and where love transcends differences to create deep connections. These aren't lofty ideals; they are the building blocks of heaven made tangible. They are what make a utopia possible, not in some far-off paradise but right here among us.

A utopian society is one where divine wisdom shapes how we live, work, and interact. It's a world where resources are shared equitably, where the vulnerable are protected, and where creativity and collaboration flourish. This vision challenges us to rethink our priorities and structures. Are we building systems that foster compassion and justice, or are we perpetuating ones that exploit and divide? Heaven on earth is not a passive gift; it's a collective effort that requires intentional choices. It asks us to shift our focus from individual gain to the common good, from scarcity to abundance, and from exclusion to inclusion.

The idea that utopia is available to us now doesn't mean the world will suddenly become perfect. Suffering, conflict, and imperfection are part of the human experience. But what it does mean is that we have the tools to transform our world into something closer to divine intent. Every act of kindness, every step toward fairness, and every moment of selfless love contributes to this transformation. Utopia is not about eliminating all challenges but about creating a world where those challenges are met with courage, support, and a shared commitment to the greater good.

The work of bringing heaven to earth is deeply practical. It involves caring for the environment, advocating for justice, and building communities where everyone feels valued and safe. It's about teaching children the importance of empathy and standing up for those who are marginalized. It's about finding joy in shared meals, offering forgiveness when it's hard, and celebrating the beauty of diversity. These small, everyday actions are the seeds of utopia. They remind us that heaven is not somewhere else. It's here, in the way we choose to live and love.

This perspective changes how we think about faith and spirituality. They are no longer just personal journeys or preparations for an afterlife. They become blueprints for creating heaven in the here and now. Faith is about action, about living in a way that reflects divine wisdom in tangible ways. Spirituality becomes a communal endeavor, a shared commitment to building a world where the values of heaven, the values of love, justice, and compassion, are evident in everything we do. Utopia is not a dream; it's a call to action. It's a reminder that heaven is not a destination we travel to but a reality we can build together.

The Evolution Of Faith

Faith is a living and evolving part of a believer's spiritual journey. In biblical mythology, this dynamic nature of faith is a central theme, illustrating how it is meant to grow and adapt as individuals deepen their understanding of the divine. Faith is not static; it is expected to expand with time, experience, and reflection. This growth is not solely the result of human effort but is nurtured and guided by the holy spirit, a force that inspires and sustains believers as they navigate their spiritual paths.

The journey of faith begins with a seed of belief, a spark of trust in something greater than oneself. This initial faith often grows through experiences of love, forgiveness, or a sense of divine presence in moments of difficulty or joy. As believers encounter challenges, their faith can be tested and refined, much like precious metals are purified in fire. These moments are not meant to break them but to strengthen their understanding and reliance on divine wisdom.

In biblical mythology, the holy spirit acts as a helper and guide, offering believers insight and comfort as they wrestle with doubt, confusion, or fear. This nurturing presence allows faith to become more resilient and deeply rooted, especially during times of uncertainty. The spirit encourages believers to explore their spiritual questions, fostering an environment where faith is not blind or unquestioning but thoughtful and informed.

Faith's evolution is not just about personal growth. It is also about how it manifests in the world through actions and relationships. As believers mature in their faith, they are called to embody its principles in tangible ways. Acts of kindness, justice, and compassion are outward signs of an inward transformation. This lived faith demonstrates that spiritual growth is not an abstract concept but a reality that shapes every aspect of life.

Biblical mythology also shows that faith's dynamic nature includes room for struggle and imperfection. Figures like Abraham, Moses, and Peter experienced moments of doubt, fear, or failure. These struggles did not disqualify them from their spiritual journeys. Instead, they became opportunities for growth and deeper connection with the divine. The acknowledgment of these imperfections reminds believers that faith is not about achieving perfection but about pursuing an authentic relationship with god.

The dynamic nature of faith underscores that spiritual growth is a continuous process. It invites believers to engage fully with their beliefs, explore their doubts, and live out their convictions in meaningful ways. This journey is both deeply personal and profoundly communal, showing that faith's evolution enriches individual lives and contributes to a more compassionate and just world.

The Call To Discipleship

Discipleship is at the heart of the spiritual journey for believers, offering a profound way to understand and live out divine wisdom. It is not just about learning; it is about forging a relationship that transforms both the mind and the heart. Discipleship is rooted in a deep commitment to follow and embody the teachings of the divine as demonstrated in the life of Jesus Christ. In biblical mythology, discipleship is less about blind adherence and more about a personal and evolving connection with god's truth.

The concept of discipleship shines brightly in the Gospels, where Jesus extended a simple yet life-changing invitation to those around him: "Follow me." This invitation was not limited to any specific group. It crossed boundaries of class, profession, and personal history. Fishermen, tax collectors, and outcasts all found themselves called into a relationship where learning from Jesus became the centerpiece of their lives. This relationship demanded more than intellectual understanding; it required a willingness to grow, change, and align one's actions with divine principles.

At its core, discipleship involves a relationship of trust and learning between the disciple and the teacher. The disciples of Jesus were not just students who absorbed information; they were participants in a way of life. They witnessed how divine wisdom could transform the brokenhearted, challenge injustice, and bring healing to the world. In following Jesus, they learned to embrace love, compassion, and humility as guiding principles. This was not an abstract or theoretical exercise. It was deeply practical, grounded in the reality of serving others and striving for justice.

The progression of discipleship mirrors the growth of faith itself. It begins with a spark of curiosity or belief, grows through experiences of learning and serving, and matures into a deeper understanding of divine wisdom. This growth is not linear or without struggle. It often involves moments of doubt, failure, and questioning. Yet, these moments are not signs of failure in discipleship; they are opportunities for transformation. The holy spirit plays an essential role in guiding disciples through these challenges, offering wisdom and encouragement when the path feels uncertain.

The teachings of Jesus in biblical mythology reflect the relational and transformative nature of discipleship. He did not simply impart knowledge. He demonstrated a way of life, showing his followers how to embody divine values in their actions. He challenged them to go beyond legalistic interpretations of the Law and to embrace its deeper intent, which was always rooted in love and justice. Discipleship, then, is not about rigid adherence to rules. It is about aligning one's life with the values of the divine and letting those values guide every decision and action.

Discipleship is not static or confined to a specific stage of life. It is a lifelong journey that grows as faith deepens and wisdom expands. It requires humility, a willingness to learn, and an openness to change. This journey is not undertaken alone. The communal aspect of discipleship is vital, as believers support and encourage one another in their shared pursuit of divine wisdom. Together, they create a community where love and justice are lived out, reflecting the teachings of Jesus and the values of god.

The Call To Apostleship

Apostleship is a powerful progression in the journey of faith. It takes the foundational aspects of discipleship, the aspects of learning, following, and growing, and elevates them to a new level of responsibility and purpose. While discipleship focuses on personal transformation and understanding, apostleship shifts the focus outward. It calls individuals to take the divine wisdom they have learned and share it with the world, becoming living representations of the divine message they carry. This transition reflects a deeper maturity of faith and a readiness to step into the role of an emissary of god's values.

In biblical mythology, the apostleship of Jesus's followers marked a turning point in their spiritual journeys. These individuals had walked alongside him, learned from his teachings, and witnessed his actions. Yet, their calling did not stop there. Jesus tasked them with a mission to go out into the world and spread the message of love, justice, and salvation. This commission, often referred to as the Great Commission, was not just a call to teach or preach. It was an invitation to embody and enact the divine message in every corner of society. Apostleship was never about staying within the comfort of what was known. It was about venturing into unfamiliar and even hostile environments to share the transformative power of divine wisdom.

Apostleship demands an unwavering commitment to the values of the divine. Apostles are not merely messengers; they are ambassadors whose lives reflect the message they carry. In biblical mythology, this role came with significant challenges. The apostles faced rejection, persecution, and immense personal sacrifice. Their journey was not about seeking comfort or safety but about dedicating themselves fully to a mission that transcended personal concerns. Their experiences highlight that apostleship is not an easy path. It is a calling that requires courage, resilience, and faith in the face of adversity.

One of the most compelling aspects of apostleship is its emphasis on action. It is not enough to understand or believe in the divine message. Apostleship calls for tangible expressions of that belief in how one interacts with the world. This could mean advocating for justice, caring for the marginalized, or challenging systems of oppression. In the New Testament, the apostles did not merely speak about the love of god. They demonstrated it through their actions, whether by healing the sick, feeding the hungry, or standing up to corrupt authorities. Their example serves as a reminder that apostleship is deeply tied to living out faith in practical and meaningful ways.

Apostleship also underscores the communal nature of the faith journey. While discipleship often focuses on personal growth, apostleship expands the scope to include the collective responsibility of building a community that reflects god's values. The apostles worked together, supporting one another as they carried out their mission. Their collective efforts laid the foundation for what would become the early church. This aspect of apostleship shows that the work of spreading divine wisdom is not an isolated endeavor. It is a shared mission that thrives on collaboration, mutual encouragement, and a sense of shared purpose.

The progression from discipleship to apostleship also highlights the evolving nature of faith. It is a reminder that faith is not meant to remain static. As one grows in understanding and commitment, the responsibilities of faith grow as well. Apostleship represents a deep trust from god, entrusting individuals with the task of representing divine wisdom to the world. It is both an honor and a challenge, requiring a level of spiritual maturity that is rooted in humility and a genuine love for others.

Apostleship invites believers to see themselves as active participants in the unfolding of divine wisdom in the world. It calls for a faith that is not just personal but also outward-facing, aimed at making a tangible difference. It is a powerful reminder that the divine message is not meant to be kept within the confines of personal experience but is meant to be shared, lived, and brought into the broader human story. In this way, apostleship becomes a transformative force, shaping not only the lives of those who take on the role but also the communities and societies they touch.

The Spiritual Journey

Eidotheosophy takes a different view from traditional doctrines on the idea of apostolic succession. Instead of seeing spiritual authority passed down through an unbroken chain of church leaders, it frames the spiritual journey as a deeply personal evolution that unfolds naturally in phases. These phases, the believer, the disciple, and the apostle, represent stages of growth that are accessible to anyone who seeks spiritual understanding. This perspective shifts the focus from institutional authority to individual transformation.

The phase of the believer is where most spiritual journeys begin. It's the point where someone acknowledges their faith, however tentative or uncertain that faith might be. In biblical mythology, we see examples of this in people who encounter god or Jesus for the first time. These are moments of awakening, where an individual begins to recognize something larger than themselves. In this phase, the focus is often inward, as people seek to understand their beliefs and how those beliefs fit into their lives. There's no pressure to have all the answers or to follow a rigid structure. It's a phase of exploration and self-discovery.

As the journey continues, some may naturally progress into the phase of the disciple. This is a stage marked by learning and commitment. In biblical mythology, disciples are portrayed as those who actively follow, learn, and try to embody the teachings of Jesus. The emphasis here is on growth, both spiritually and ethically. It's not about blind obedience but about understanding and applying spiritual principles in everyday life. The disciple is still a student, but there's a shift from internal reflection to outward action. People in this phase start to consider how their beliefs can positively impact their behaviour and relationships with others.

For those who feel called to go further, the phase of the apostle represents a stage of leadership and service. Apostles, as depicted in biblical mythology, are not just followers; they are messengers and agents of change. They take what they've learned and use it to inspire and support others. This phase isn't limited to a select few chosen by a hierarchy. Eidotheosophy rejects the idea that apostleship is exclusive or that it requires formal validation. Instead, it sees apostleship as a natural progression for anyone who feels compelled to share and apply their spiritual growth in a broader context. Apostleship in this sense is not about power or authority. It's about responsibility and the desire to make a difference.

By framing the spiritual journey this way, eidotheosophy emphasizes personal agency and growth over institutional control. Apostolic succession, as traditionally understood, ties spiritual leadership to formal hierarchies and the idea that certain individuals are uniquely qualified to carry forward divine authority. This creates barriers that separate clergy from laypeople and reinforces the notion that spiritual leadership is a privilege reserved for the few. Eidotheosophy dismantles this divide by affirming that every individual has the capacity to progress through these phases, guided by their own experiences, insights, and efforts.

This approach aligns with the broader message of biblical mythology, where many of the key figures were ordinary people. Jesus called fishermen, tax collectors, and others who would never have been seen as spiritual authorities in their communities. These individuals became disciples and apostles not because they were part of an elite group, but because they were willing to learn, grow, and take on the challenge of living out their beliefs. Eidotheosophy captures this spirit by making the path accessible to everyone, regardless of their background or status.

The idea of spiritual evolution also acknowledges that not everyone will follow the same path or reach the same stages at the same time. Some may feel content in the phase of the believer, finding fulfillment in their personal faith without feeling the need to move further. Others might become disciples but never feel called to apostleship. There's no hierarchy in these phases, no sense that one is better or more important than another. Each phase is valuable and meaningful in its own right.

Eidotheosophy's rejection of apostolic succession also has practical implications. It challenges the notion that spiritual authority should be centralized or controlled by institutions. This decentralization fosters a more inclusive and egalitarian approach to spirituality. It allows for a diversity of voices and experiences, enriching the collective understanding of faith. It also prevents the kind of abuses that can occur when power is concentrated in the hands of a few.

By focusing on the phases of the believer, the disciple, and the apostle, eidotheosophy offers a model of spiritual growth that is dynamic, inclusive, and deeply personal. It removes the barriers that often make spirituality feel inaccessible or hierarchical and instead invites everyone to participate in their own journey. Whether one remains a believer, becomes a disciple, or steps into apostleship, each phase is a valid and valuable expression of the spiritual experience.

Starting a faith ministry begins with an honest exploration of who you are and what you bring to the table. It is a deeply personal process that involves discovering your divine gifts and understanding your calling. These two elements are the foundation of a meaningful and effective ministry. Your gifts and calling are not random or interchangeable; they are specific to you, carefully tailored to the role you are meant to play in the broader spiritual tapestry.

Your calling is the overarching purpose that draws you forward, the mission you feel compelled to undertake. In biblical mythology, calling is central to many stories. Moses was called to lead his people out of slavery, David was called to be a shepherd-king, and Paul was called to bring the message of Christ to the Gentiles. These individuals did not stumble into their roles. They were drawn by a sense of purpose that demanded their unique abilities and perspectives. Your calling might not involve leading a nation or founding a movement, but it is no less significant. It is the specific way you are meant to make a difference, to contribute to the lives of others and reflect the divine in your work.

Your gifts are the tools you have been given to fulfill your calling. They are the talents, abilities, and strengths that come naturally to you, often with a sense of joy or fulfillment when you use them. Gifts can take many forms. Some people have a natural ability to connect with others on an emotional level, offering comfort and understanding. Others have the organizational skills to bring structure and efficiency to chaotic situations. Still others might excel in teaching, creativity, or advocacy. In biblical mythology, these gifts are seen as coming from god, entrusted to individuals for a specific purpose. The apostle Paul wrote extensively about spiritual gifts, emphasizing that every gift is valuable and that each person's contributions are necessary for the community to thrive.

Understanding your gifts requires self-reflection and sometimes the input of others. People around you often see your strengths more clearly than you do. They might notice that you have a knack for leadership or a talent for inspiring others. Pay attention to what people say when they praise your abilities. These observations can provide valuable clues about where your gifts lie. Equally important is reflecting on what brings you the most satisfaction. The activities that light you up inside often align with your gifts, because they connect you to your sense of purpose.

Your calling and gifts work hand in hand. Your calling provides the direction, while your gifts provide the means to get there. For example, if your calling involves caring for the sick, your gifts might include patience, empathy, or medical knowledge. If your calling is to teach, your gifts could include a clear way of explaining complex ideas or the ability to engage an audience. Without an understanding of your calling, your gifts might feel aimless. Without an awareness of your gifts, your calling might feel overwhelming or unattainable.

Once you have a sense of your gifts and calling, the next step is to think about how they can come together in a practical way. This is where the idea of ministry becomes tangible. Ministry is not confined to a traditional church setting. It can take place in schools, hospitals, homes, or anywhere else where people gather. Your ministry might involve mentoring young people, creating art that inspires others, or advocating for justice in your community. The possibilities are as varied as the people who feel called to serve.

Recognizing your gifts and calling is not a one-time event. It is an ongoing journey. As you grow and encounter new experiences, your understanding of yourself and your purpose will deepen. The gifts you lean on in one season of life might shift as your calling evolves. Staying open to this process allows your ministry to remain vibrant and meaningful. It also requires humility and a willingness to listen, both to the divine and to the needs of the world around you.

Your gifts and calling are essential to your ministry's success because they align you with what you are uniquely equipped to do. By focusing on your strengths and the purpose you feel most connected to, you can create a ministry that not only fulfills you but also serves others in the most effective way. When you operate out of your gifts and calling, you bring your best self to the work. You also experience a sense of alignment and peace, knowing that you are contributing in a way that is true to who you are. That authenticity is what draws people in and makes your ministry a place where lives can be transformed.

Racism

In the context of eidotheosophy, racism is a moral failure that undermines the principles of justice, equality, and the inherent worth of every individual. It's not just a social issue; it's a spiritual one. Racism creates barriers between people, feeding into systems of oppression that harm individuals and communities while distorting the values that should guide us. From the perspective of eidotheosophy, it becomes essential to not only recognize the existence of racism but to actively confront and dismantle it. This is about aligning spiritual understanding with real-world action, guided by reason, evidence, and a commitment to collective well-being.

Racism, at its core, denies the full humanity of others. It is a construct rooted in the false idea that some groups are inherently superior to others based on physical characteristics, ancestry, or cultural differences. Historical context shows how these ideas have been institutionalized, creating systems that perpetuate inequality and exclusion. From slavery and colonialism to segregation and ongoing disparities in wealth, education, and health, the legacy of racism is written into the fabric of many societies. Addressing it means grappling with both its historical roots and its present-day manifestations.

Biblical mythology has often been used to both justify and oppose racism, which illustrates the importance of careful interpretation and critical thinking. Passages have been twisted to defend slavery and segregation, yet the same texts contain principles of love, compassion, and justice that stand firmly against such practices. Eidotheosophy calls for a reevaluation of these texts, separating the wisdom that promotes unity and dignity from the human biases that have been woven into interpretations over centuries. By doing so, we can reclaim the spiritual narratives that support the idea of equality as a divine mandate.

The concept of the holy spirit, as understood within eidotheosophy, offers a powerful counter to racism. If the holy spirit represents divine influence in the world, then it must also stand for unity, compassion, and the breaking down of barriers between people. Racism, in contrast, thrives on division and fear, creating false hierarchies that undermine the collective good. Engaging with the holy spirit means rejecting these divisions and working toward a society that reflects the spiritual ideals of justice and mutual respect. It's not enough to hold these values in theory; they must be acted upon in practical, measurable ways.

Academic research provides further insight into the mechanisms of racism and how it can be dismantled. Studies have shown that systemic racism affects everything from economic opportunities to health outcomes. For instance, access to quality education and healthcare is often stratified along racial lines, perpetuating cycles of disadvantage. These disparities are not accidents; they are the result of policies and practices that can be traced, analyzed, and reformed. Confronting racism means understanding its systemic nature and committing to structural changes that address these inequalities.

Addressing racism also requires confronting its psychological and cultural dimensions. Implicit biases, which are unconscious associations and attitudes, play a significant role in perpetuating discrimination. These biases are not inherently malicious, but they can lead to harmful outcomes if left unchecked. Acknowledging their existence is the first step toward change. Education, exposure to diverse perspectives, and honest self-reflection are tools we can use to challenge these biases and build a more inclusive mindset. This work is not easy, but it is necessary if we are to create a society that reflects spiritual and ethical ideals.

Racism is not just a failure of individuals; it is a failure of systems. Laws and institutions that perpetuate inequality must be examined and reformed. This includes addressing issues like discriminatory policing practices, disparities in sentencing, and barriers to voting. It also means promoting policies that foster equity, such as fair housing laws, affirmative action, and investments in underserved communities. These changes require political will and collective action, but they are essential for creating a society that values every individual equally.

In the context of eidotheosophy, confronting racism is a spiritual mandate as much as a social one. It is about aligning our actions with the values of justice, compassion, and unity that form the foundation of a reasonable and ethical approach to faith. It is about recognizing the full humanity of others and committing to a path of healing and reconciliation. This work is ongoing, and it requires effort from all of us, regardless of our backgrounds or beliefs. By addressing racism with honesty and resolve, we can move closer to a world that reflects the ideals we hold dear.

Gender And Gender Identity

One of the most challenging and, at times, problematic aspects of biblical mythology is its treatment of gender and gender identity. The roles assigned to men and women in biblical mythology often reflect the cultural norms of the times in which the texts were written, which were patriarchal and restrictive. Men were generally seen as leaders, warriors, and prophets, while women were expected to be obedient, nurturing, and supportive. These gender roles were rigid, and the stories often reinforced the idea that men and women had fixed, separate spheres of influence and responsibility.

In the Old Testament, women's roles are frequently limited to being wives, mothers, and daughters, with their worth often tied to their relationships to men. The stories of biblical women like Eve, Sarah, Rebekah, and Esther highlight their importance in the narrative but also underscore their secondary status compared to male figures. The concept of a woman being made from a man's rib, as seen in the story of Adam and Eve, is often cited as a foundational example of biblical mythology's view of women. This creation story has been interpreted to mean that women are subordinate to men, a belief that has contributed to the long history of gender inequality within many religious traditions.

However, when you look deeper into the stories of certain biblical women, you can see that there are complex and dynamic portrayals that challenge these stereotypes. Figures like Deborah, the judge and prophet, and Jael, who played a crucial role in the defeat of the Canaanite army, show that women were not just passive or subservient. These women had significant agency, making important decisions and taking actions that impacted the course of history. But these stories are often overshadowed by the more dominant, male-centered narratives, which sometimes leads to the marginalization of these women's contributions.

There's also the issue of how biblical texts have been used historically to justify the oppression of women. The writings of Paul, particularly in the New Testament, have often been quoted to limit women's roles within the church and society. Passages like 1 Timothy 2:12, which states that women should not teach or have authority over men, have been used to argue for women's submission. These texts have been controversial for centuries, as they seem to contradict the more progressive teachings of Jesus, who often elevated the status of women, treating them with dignity and respect.

But beyond the binary understanding of gender, biblical mythology offers a more nuanced view in some cases. The story of creation in Genesis, for example, states that both man and woman were made in god's image, a statement that suggests equality and dignity for both. In the New Testament, Paul writes in Galatians 3:28, "There is neither Jew nor Greek, slave nor free, male nor female, for you are all one in Christ Jesus." This line speaks to the potential for a more inclusive and egalitarian community, one that transcends the limitations of gender, race, and status. It challenges the notion that one gender is superior to the other, opening the door for a broader understanding of equality.

When it comes to gender identity, biblical mythology doesn't directly address the modern concept of transgender or non-binary identities. The idea of gender being a spectrum or something that can shift or exist outside of the male/female binary was not part of the cultural understanding at the time the texts were written. As a result, biblical mythology does not provide clear guidance on how to navigate these identities. Yet, the overarching principles of love, acceptance, and dignity for all people can still be applied to discussions around gender identity. Jesus' teachings focused on loving your neighbor as yourself and treating others with respect and kindness. These values could serve as a foundation for a more inclusive view of gender diversity, even if the specific language of biblical mythology doesn't directly address it.

In recent years, many theologians and religious scholars have begun re-examining these texts, seeking to reconcile the more problematic aspects of biblical mythology with a more inclusive and equitable view of gender. Some argue that biblical mythology's message of love, justice, and compassion should be applied in a way that affirms the dignity of all people, regardless of gender or gender identity. These conversations are still unfolding, but they reflect a broader trend in contemporary religious thought to challenge traditional interpretations and push for a more inclusive understanding of scripture.

There is also an important conversation around how biblical mythology's portrayal of gender impacts the way people understand their own identity. For many, the biblical narrative shapes their perception of what it means to be a man or a woman, sometimes leading to internal conflict when one's experience of gender doesn't align with the traditional expectations. The challenge for many believers today is how to reconcile their faith with their understanding of gender and identity, especially in a world where gender roles are increasingly fluid and inclusive. The tension between ancient texts and modern experiences can be difficult to navigate, but it is also an opportunity for growth and deeper understanding of what it means to live in accordance with divine wisdom.

Gender Identity

Divine wisdom, as portrayed in biblical mythology, can be seen as supportive of diverse gender identities, even if the traditional interpretations of scripture have not always aligned with this understanding. Biblical mythology, particularly when viewed through a lens of divine wisdom, speaks to the inherent value and dignity of every individual, regardless of gender or gender identity. While the historical and cultural context of the biblical texts was largely binary in its understanding of gender, the underlying principles of love, respect, and inclusivity can still offer a foundation for affirming diverse gender identities.

In the creation story of Genesis, both man and woman are created in the image of god. The idea that humanity, in its fullness, reflects the divine nature speaks to a vision of equality and completeness that transcends gender. When god creates humankind in god's image, it is a declaration of inherent worth, not defined by a specific gender or role but rather by the essence of being human. While Genesis primarily frames this creation as male and female, it also leaves room for the understanding that gender identity is more complex and multifaceted than the binary system traditionally upheld.

In a broader spiritual context, divine wisdom is not limited to a rigid understanding of gender roles. Throughout biblical mythology, the focus is on the heart, character, and relationship with the divine. Many of the figures in biblical mythology, both male and female, break free from the confines of their gender roles to fulfill their divine calling. Deborah, the prophetess and judge, serves as a powerful example of how god's wisdom transcends gender expectations. Her role as a leader and decision-maker shows that divine wisdom empowers individuals to rise above societal constraints and fulfill their purpose, regardless of their gender.

Jesus' interactions with women are also pivotal in understanding the inclusive nature of divine wisdom. Throughout the Gospels, Jesus speaks with, heals, and supports women in ways that were considered radical for the time. His approach upended the traditional patriarchal norms and demonstrated that the value of a person is not determined by their gender but by their capacity to love, serve, and live in alignment with divine wisdom. Jesus never discriminated based on gender, and many of his followers, including women, played vital roles in spreading his message.

The teachings of Paul, often cited as reinforcing traditional gender roles, can also be reinterpreted in light of divine wisdom. While some of Paul's letters have been used to justify the subordination of women, his writings also contain affirmations of equality and unity in Christ. For instance, in Galatians 3:28, Paul writes, "There is neither Jew nor Greek, slave nor free, male nor female, for you are all one in Christ Jesus." This passage underscores the idea that the divine plan is not limited by human distinctions, including gender. When viewed through the lens of divine wisdom, this message encourages a more inclusive and accepting view of gender diversity.

Furthermore, divine wisdom, in its purest form, calls for compassion, understanding, and acceptance. The concept of agape, or unconditional love, central to Christian teaching, suggests that love should extend to all people, regardless of gender identity. When we embrace this kind of love, we are not only accepting the person but also recognizing the divinity within them. It is this divine wisdom that can support individuals in expressing their authentic gender identity without fear of rejection or discrimination.

As society's understanding of gender evolves, so too can our interpretation of biblical wisdom. In light of contemporary discussions on gender identity, divine wisdom can be understood as encouraging acceptance of the full spectrum of human experience. Biblical mythology does not need to be in conflict with the affirmation of diverse gender identities; rather, the principles of love, justice, and compassion can guide us toward a more inclusive interpretation that honours all people, regardless of their gender identity. In this way, divine wisdom does not condemn or limit but rather supports the flourishing of all individuals as they live into the fullness of their identity.

Ultimately, divine wisdom offers a path toward acceptance, where gender diversity is not only tolerated but embraced as part of the divine plan. The idea that every person is made in the image of god, and that their worth is not defined by societal expectations but by their inherent value as a creation of the divine, opens up space for a more inclusive and compassionate understanding of gender. As we grow in wisdom and understanding, we can begin to see that divine wisdom truly supports diverse gender identities and that all people, regardless of gender, are equally loved and valued by the divine.

Sexuality In Biblical Mythology

One area of particular contention in biblical mythology is the way the teachings on sex and sexuality have been interpreted and used to justify discrimination and harm against LGBTQ+ people. Throughout history, certain passages have been used to condemn same-sex relationships, often misinterpreting the deeper messages that biblical mythology presents. Many of these interpretations are rooted in a limited and often culturally specific understanding of human sexuality that does not account for the diversity of sexual and gender identities that exist. When we read these scriptures with divine wisdom in mind, we begin to see that the messages about love, justice, and inclusion are much more central than the rigid categories often imposed by traditional interpretations.

The most commonly cited passages used to condemn LGBTQ+ people are from Leviticus 18:22 and 20:13, which state that "you shall not lie with a man as with a woman" and "if a man has relations with a man as one does with a woman, both of them have done what is detestable." These verses have been used to justify exclusion and harm against LGBTQ+ individuals. However, when viewed within their historical and cultural context, these verses were part of a larger set of laws that were specifically about ritual purity and community standards for the Israelites. The laws were not necessarily meant to be applied universally or for all time, and certainly not to the experiences of individuals today. They reflected the cultural norms of the time, which were deeply influenced by ancient views on gender roles and sexuality that are vastly different from those of modern society.

The idea that these verses should be understood as universally applicable to all people, across time and culture, ignores the way that biblical mythology often deals with cultural practices and customs that were unique to specific historical moments. When we look at the overarching message of biblical mythology, it is clear that the focus is on love, justice, and the treatment of others with respect. Jesus' teachings emphasize love for one another, even for one's enemies, and call us to create a community where everyone is accepted and treated with dignity, regardless of their background or identity.

Biblical mythology speaks much more directly about issues of justice and mercy than about specific sexual practices. For example, the New Testament highlights how Jesus interacted with marginalized groups, such as women, the poor, and the sick. He focused on showing love and acceptance, rather than condemnation, to those who were often pushed to the fringes of society. These messages are far more important in understanding the heart of biblical mythology and its call for believers to love one another. The apostle Paul, often cited in arguments against LGBTQ+ people, also wrote extensively about love and equality, famously stating in Galatians 3:28 that "there is neither Jew nor Greek, slave nor free, male nor female, for you are all one in Christ Jesus." This passage, which emphasizes the fundamental equality of all people, can easily be extended to include LGBTQ+ individuals as well.

Ultimately, biblical mythology is not meant to be a tool for exclusion or discrimination. When we look at the broader message of divine wisdom, we see that it calls us to love one another, to seek justice, and to show mercy. The teachings on sex and sexuality, when interpreted through this lens, should not be used as a justification for harm or exclusion. Instead, they should be understood as part of a larger call to live lives of compassion, understanding, and inclusivity. Discrimination against LGBTQ+ people, based on narrow and often outdated interpretations of scripture, does not align with the core principles of the biblical message, which is rooted in love and justice for all.

Throughout history, biblical mythology has often been criticized for allegedly endorsing slavery and the exploitation of workers. Many have pointed to certain passages in the biblical texts that seem to condone or regulate slavery as proof of a divine endorsement of such practices. However, when examined more closely, these texts do not promote slavery in the way that some might assume. Instead, they provide a framework for how slaves should be treated, showing that the core principles of biblical mythology actually emphasize the inherent dignity and value of every human being.

The idea of slavery in biblical mythology, especially in the Old Testament, is often seen through the lens of the ancient world. Slavery was a widespread institution in many societies, and biblical mythology reflects that reality. However, the laws and guidelines found in the texts do not promote or celebrate the practice; rather, they serve as a form of regulation to mitigate its abuses. For example, in the book of Exodus, the laws governing the treatment of slaves were designed to protect them, providing a form of care and compassion not typically seen in other ancient cultures. In fact, one of the key principles in biblical mythology is that all people, including slaves, are created in the image of god and, therefore, should be treated with respect and dignity.

The concept of work in biblical mythology also plays a significant role in how workers are to be treated. While the text doesn't explicitly condemn slavery as we understand it today, it does provide a strong moral framework for how people should be treated in their work relationships. The famous commandment to "love your neighbor as yourself" is one of the fundamental ethical principles that guides how workers should be treated, implying that their worth is not based on their status or role but on their humanity. This guiding principle offers a moral critique of any exploitation or mistreatment in the workplace, pointing to the idea that work should be dignified and fair.

Furthermore, the New Testament echoes this idea, especially through the teachings of Jesus. In his ministry, Jesus consistently uplifted the marginalized, including workers and the poor. His actions, such as washing the feet of his disciples, were demonstrations of servant leadership, showing that those in positions of authority have a responsibility to care for and serve those beneath them. The apostle Paul also emphasizes the value of equitable treatment in the workplace, encouraging employers to treat their workers justly and fairly, recognizing that both employer and employee are equal in the eyes of god.

While it is true that biblical mythology contains some passages that have been historically misused to justify the exploitation of workers, a careful reading shows that the overarching message is one of justice, compassion, and respect for the dignity of every individual. These teachings provide the foundation for a more humane and ethical treatment of workers, encouraging employers and society at large to uphold the inherent worth of each person.

Biblical mythology offers profound insights into the nature of life, health, and well-being. Despite the common misconception that it places exclusive emphasis on spiritual matters and dismisses the importance of mental and physical health services, biblical mythology presents a much broader perspective. It emphasizes that human beings are whole beings, with both physical and spiritual needs. The idea that prayer alone is enough to address all aspects of health is not supported by the texts themselves. In fact, biblical mythology acknowledges the necessity of taking care of one's body, mind, and spirit.

Throughout biblical mythology, we see numerous examples of people seeking help for their physical and mental health challenges. For instance, in the Old Testament, there are instances where people seek the help of physicians for healing, showing that even in ancient times, the importance of professional medical care was recognized. In the New Testament, Jesus is portrayed as both a healer and a teacher, but he never dismisses the need for other forms of care. He heals people of their ailments, but this is not presented as a replacement for the need for practical care, but rather as an expression of divine compassion.

Additionally, the teachings of biblical mythology are full of practical wisdom on maintaining physical and mental well-being. Proverbs, for example, is rich with advice on how to live a balanced life, taking care of your body, eating healthily, and living wisely. There's also an underlying message that our bodies are temples, which can be understood as a call to respect and care for our physical health. The idea that we are to honor the body and treat it with dignity aligns with the understanding that neglecting mental or physical health is not in line with divine wisdom.

Furthermore, the biblical mythological view on mental health is also often misunderstood. Far from discouraging individuals from seeking help when struggling mentally or emotionally, biblical mythology is full of examples of people wrestling with their emotions and seeking guidance. Many of the psalms express deep sorrow, anxiety, and distress, offering a space for the acknowledgment of mental and emotional struggles. At no point does biblical mythology suggest that these feelings should be ignored or simply prayed away. Rather, it encourages believers to express their struggles, seek counsel, and understand that healing may come in many forms.

In biblical mythology, we also see the importance of community in healing. The early Christian church, for example, was a community that supported one another in times of need. The communal aspect of well-being is central to biblical mythology, highlighting that people are meant to help one another through both spiritual and practical means. It is not an either/or situation; the spiritual and physical realms work together in the pursuit of a whole, healthy life.

Ultimately, biblical mythology does not present a dichotomy between spiritual and physical or mental health. Instead, it promotes a holistic approach where all aspects of human well-being are valued. Prayer and faith seem to be important parts of this process, but they are not substitutes for seeking out necessary physical and mental health services. The message of biblical mythology, when understood correctly, encourages people to care for their whole being, their spirit, mind, and body.

The concept of marriage must be examined through the lens of its real-world impacts rather than metaphysical claims. Many faith traditions present marriage as a divine institution, often described as unbreakable and central to fulfilling spiritual mandates like procreation. These ideas are woven deeply into biblical mythology, which frequently upholds marriage as a covenant not just between two individuals but also between them and god. However, when we step back from these spiritual assertions, it becomes clear that marriage, as it exists in many societies, has evolved into a system that too often violates women's autonomy, perpetuates abuse, and sustains structural inequities.

The permanence of marriage is a recurring theme in biblical mythology. Passages like "what god has joined together, let no one separate" have been interpreted to mean that marriage is divinely ordained and irrevocable. This belief has been used to stigmatize divorce and keep partners, primarily women, trapped in harmful relationships. It ignores the reality that some marriages are marred by emotional, physical, or financial abuse. When women are coerced to remain in such marriages due to religious or societal pressures, the system actively perpetuates harm. It transforms what should be a partnership into a prison, where autonomy and personal safety are sacrificed at the altar of spiritual permanence.

The expectation of reproduction as a fundamental purpose of marriage further highlights the tension between metaphysical concerns and real-world consequences. Biblical mythology often ties marriage to the command to "be fruitful and multiply," framing childbearing as both a duty and a divine blessing. While this might have made sense in historical contexts where population growth was essential for community survival, it becomes problematic when imposed as a universal mandate. It disregards the fact that not all individuals or couples wish to have children, are able to do so, or are in a position to provide a safe and nurturing environment. Forcing this expectation on women, in particular, reduces their role within marriage to that of a reproductive vessel, stripping them of agency over their own bodies.

Marriage systems have also historically been used to reinforce patriarchal structures. In many traditions, women are seen as subordinate to their husbands, both legally and socially. Biblical mythology includes passages that instruct women to "submit" to their husbands, creating a dynamic where male dominance is not just normalized but sanctified. This framework has often been used to justify the unequal treatment of women, including their exclusion from decision-making within the family and society at large. It sustains cycles of inequality, where women are taught from a young age that their worth is tied to their ability to marry and serve a husband, rather than their individual talents, aspirations, and choices.

Abuse within marriage is another critical issue. The institution of marriage has too often been weaponized to excuse or hide abuse. Religious and cultural norms that prioritize the preservation of marriage above all else frequently discourage victims, primarily women, from seeking help or leaving abusive partners. In some cases, the abuser is shielded by the belief that their actions are private matters to be resolved within the sanctity of marriage. This approach not only fails to protect victims but also perpetuates cycles of harm, as abusers face no real accountability.

Eidotheosophy rejects the notion that marriage, or any human institution, should be immune from scrutiny simply because it is linked to spiritual or divine claims. Instead, it calls for an evaluation of marriage based on its actual outcomes. Does the institution as it currently exists promote equity, respect, and mutual well-being? Or does it create environments where harm is excused and injustice thrives? For rational believers, these questions are far more important than metaphysical assertions about the divine nature of marriage.

If marriage continues to perpetuate systems that cause harm, it must be reimagined or, in some cases, abandoned altogether. While the idea of a committed partnership can hold value for many people, it should not come at the expense of autonomy or safety. Partnerships should be built on mutual respect, equal decision-making, and the freedom to leave if the relationship no longer serves both individuals' well-being. This approach would move away from the rigid structures often upheld by traditional marriage systems and toward a model that prioritizes human dignity and flourishing.

Eidotheosophy invites us to let go of the assumption that marriage, as defined by biblical mythology or tradition, is inherently good or necessary. It challenges us to ask whether the systems we uphold actually contribute to a just and equitable society. When marriage is examined without the filter of metaphysical concerns, it becomes clear that its value lies not in its divine framing but in whether or not it supports loving, respectful, and mutually beneficial relationships. Anything less fails to meet the standard of justice and reason that eidotheosophy seeks to uphold.

In the context of eidotheosophy, the debate around abortion becomes a balancing act between metaphysical beliefs and the tangible realities of human life. Movements that oppose abortion often ground their arguments in metaphysical concerns, such as the idea that an unrealized human, even at the earliest stages of development, has a divine right to life or that terminating a pregnancy constitutes an immoral act equivalent to killing. These are deeply held beliefs for many, rooted in interpretations of biblical mythology and the notion of a divine moral order. But the issue is complicated by the fact that these metaphysical claims cannot be empirically validated. They rely on faith and subjective interpretations of divine intent, which makes them inherently difficult, if not impossible, to resolve through rational discourse.

Eidotheosophy emphasizes the importance of engaging with real-world consequences when metaphysical debates reach an impasse. If we cannot definitively determine whether an unrealized human possesses a divine right to life, we must shift our focus to the outcomes of our actions in the physical world. From this perspective, the question becomes less about abstract moral principles and more about the tangible impact of allowing or withholding abortion on individuals and society as a whole. What are the measurable effects of restricting access to abortion on women's lives, autonomy, and well-being? What societal consequences arise from these policies, and how do they align with the values we claim to uphold?

When we examine the real-world consequences, it becomes clear that restricting abortion often results in significant harm. Denying access to abortion can endanger women's lives, particularly in cases of medical emergencies where continuing a pregnancy poses severe health risks. Historical accounts and contemporary data both show that when abortion is inaccessible, unsafe practices tend to rise, leading to increased maternal mortality and morbidity. These are not hypothetical outcomes, they are documented realities that highlight the dangers of prioritizing metaphysical concerns over practical considerations. The argument that life is sacred loses its meaning if policies enacted to preserve one form of life recklessly endanger another.

Beyond physical health, withholding abortion infringes on women's autonomy and perpetuates systems of oppression. The ability to make decisions about one's body is a fundamental aspect of personal freedom. Denying women this choice reinforces patriarchal structures that view women primarily as vessels for reproduction rather than autonomous individuals with rights and agency. It reduces their lives to a means to an end, often dictated by societal or religious expectations rather than their own needs or desires. This undermines the very principles of justice and equality that many anti-abortion movements claim to uphold.

The social and economic ramifications are just as significant. Forcing someone to carry an unwanted pregnancy to term can lead to financial hardship, limit educational and career opportunities, and perpetuate cycles of poverty. These outcomes extend beyond the individual to affect families, communities, and society at large. Policies that restrict abortion often disproportionately harm marginalized groups, including low-income individuals and people of colour, who are less likely to have access to the resources needed to navigate the barriers created by such restrictions. These are not abstract moral dilemmas; they are concrete injustices with far-reaching consequences.

Eidotheosophy encourages us to evaluate such complex issues through a lens of reason and evidence. While metaphysical concerns about the sanctity of life are deeply meaningful to many, they cannot provide a definitive guide for policy or ethical decision-making. Instead, we must consider the tangible outcomes of our actions and their alignment with the values of compassion, justice, and the well-being of all individuals. If the purpose of spirituality is to guide us toward a more just and equitable world, then policies that cause measurable harm to women and perpetuate systemic injustices cannot be reconciled with that goal.

This approach does not dismiss the significance of metaphysical beliefs but rather places them in their proper context. Beliefs about the soul, divine rights, or moral absolutes are deeply personal and meaningful, but they cannot override the lived realities of others. Rational believers, guided by the principles of eidotheosophy, recognize that true morality is grounded in the real-world impact of our choices. Protecting women's health, autonomy, and dignity must take precedence over metaphysical arguments that cannot be universally agreed upon. In this framework, the question of abortion becomes less about abstract moral absolutes and more about creating a society where all individuals are treated with respect, compassion, and fairness.

Fighting For Justice

Fighting for justice is sometimes necessary and morally justifiable, even though nonviolent methods should always be the first approach. There are moments in history when peaceful protests and diplomatic efforts have failed to stop injustice, and in these cases, taking a stand, even through force if necessary, can become the only viable way to achieve a just and equitable outcome. Biblical mythology has a clear message about the importance of standing up against oppression and fighting for the rights of the marginalized and vulnerable. It reminds us that justice is not optional, but essential, and that sometimes, to protect those who cannot protect themselves, we must be willing to take action, even when it requires great personal sacrifice or difficulty.

A striking example from biblical mythology is the life of Jesus. His ministry was rooted in the idea of justice, especially for those on the margins of society. While Jesus is often depicted as a figure of peace, there were times when he did not shy away from conflict. One of the most notable moments is when he drove the money changers out of the temple. This was not an act of violence but it was a fierce stand against corruption and exploitation. He was willing to take direct action in defence of those being wronged. Jesus' actions show us that standing for justice sometimes means challenging systems of power, even if it involves discomfort or opposition.

The prophets also provide strong examples of the necessity of fighting for justice. Throughout the Old Testament, the prophets spoke out against the oppression of the poor, the exploitation of the weak, and the corruption of leaders. Their words were often confrontational, and their actions sometimes involved standing up to powerful rulers or systems. The prophets knew that the status quo was unjust, and they were not afraid to speak truth to power, even when it meant personal peril. This speaks to the importance of actively seeking justice and being willing to confront and dismantle systems that oppress and harm others.

What we see in these examples is that biblical mythology does not shy away from the idea that fighting for justice is sometimes necessary. It doesn't offer a false ideal of passive acceptance of injustice but instead calls for a proactive stance. It calls for standing up when others are being harmed, for speaking truth to power, and for fighting for the rights and dignity of those who are vulnerable. This is a moral calling, one that demands courage, strength, and a willingness to face difficult challenges. Nonviolence should always be the first choice, but when faced with overwhelming injustice, fighting for what is right is not only justifiable but required.

In exceptional circumstances, such as when entire nations are the purveyors of harm and injustice, the call to justice can demand even more drastic action. In the case of genocide or other atrocities where a state or governing power is actively perpetrating violence against its own people or other nations, the pursuit of justice may require going to war. When such grave injustices are occurring, the international community or other nations must step in to stop the violence and protect those who are being harmed. In these extreme cases, fighting in a war or supporting forces that seek to end the injustice may be not just morally justifiable but a necessity.

Take, for example, the atrocities committed during the Holocaust in World War II. The Nazi regime engaged in the systematic extermination of millions of people. The world could not simply stand by and hope for a peaceful resolution. In this case, war became the means through which justice could be pursued and the suffering could be stopped. The Allies, despite the horrors of war, had to fight to protect those who were being annihilated. In this context, the moral imperative to protect life and defend the innocent took precedence over the choice of nonviolence. This does not mean that war is an ideal or the first choice. Rather, it underscores that in certain situations, when all other avenues for peace and justice have been exhausted, war may become a tragic but necessary response.

The same logic applies in modern conflicts where oppressive regimes or terrorist organizations engage in acts of violence, persecution, or genocide. The international community must consider the moral imperative to stop such violence, even if it means resorting to military intervention. Whether one personally chooses to fight in such a war or supports those who are working to redress the injustice may depend upon one's personal convictions. Some may feel called to join the effort, while others may choose to support the cause in different ways, such as through humanitarian aid or diplomatic pressure. But the fundamental message remains the same: when the perpetration of evil is so vast and widespread that it threatens the very lives of innocent people, military intervention may be the only way to stop it.

The biblical teachings remind us that we are not passive bystanders in the face of injustice but active participants in the pursuit of a world where everyone's rights are respected and protected. In exceptional circumstances, the call to fight for justice might even demand that we take part in a war, if that is what it takes to stop widespread harm and oppression. While the desire for peace and reconciliation should always guide our actions, we must also be prepared to stand firm against evil, wherever it is found, and to use every means necessary to protect the innocent and uphold justice.

Poverty has always been a profound and pressing issue, touching every corner of the world and shaping the lives of countless individuals and families. Its reach is vast, influencing health, education, opportunities, and even how communities function. Biblical mythology addresses this deeply human struggle with consistent and powerful calls to care for the poor and uplift those burdened by economic hardship. Across its texts, a recurring theme emerges; a divine imperative to pursue justice and extend compassion to the most vulnerable among us.

One of the clearest illustrations of this concern can be found in the laws and practices outlined in the ancient texts. The concept of gleaning, for example, provided a framework for addressing poverty in agricultural societies. Landowners were instructed not to harvest every last bit of their crops but to leave the edges of their fields unharvested for the poor and the foreigner. This practice, mentioned in Leviticus and Deuteronomy, was not a token gesture. It was a deliberate way of embedding care for the poor into the very fabric of daily life. It ensured that even in a subsistence economy, those who lacked resources could find a means of survival. This was more than charity; it was justice, acknowledging that society had a collective responsibility to ensure no one was left entirely destitute.

The prophetic books amplify this focus on justice and equity. Prophets like Amos and Isaiah were unflinching in their critique of societies that allowed the wealthy to exploit the poor or that tolerated systems of inequality. Amos's words are particularly striking. He accuses those who "trample on the poor and take from them levies of grain" while living in luxury. His rebuke is clear: a society that permits such disparity betrays its moral foundation. Isaiah, too, warns against the consequences of neglecting justice for the oppressed, calling on people to "seek justice, correct oppression, bring justice to the fatherless, and plead the widow's cause." These are not abstract ideals. They are urgent calls to action, insisting that faith must translate into tangible care for the marginalized.

The wisdom literature also reflects this concern. Proverbs, for instance, frequently ties generosity to righteousness and blessing. One verse notes that "whoever is generous to the poor lends to the Lord, and he will repay him for his deed." This framing makes an important point: caring for the poor is not optional or secondary. It is a direct expression of one's relationship with the divine. The act of helping those in need is elevated to a sacred duty, a way of aligning oneself with divine values.

The teachings attributed to Jesus in the Gospels carry this thread forward with even greater urgency. Jesus consistently prioritizes the poor and marginalized in his ministry. In one of his most famous teachings, the Sermon on the Mount, he declares, "Blessed are the poor in spirit, for theirs is the kingdom of heaven." his parables, too, often highlight the dignity of the downtrodden and the moral imperative to help them. The story of the Good Samaritan is a timeless reminder that true compassion knows no boundaries. Jesus does not merely encourage charity. He challenges his followers to dismantle the barriers that prevent people from living with dignity and to see the poor as equals, deserving of justice and care.

historically, these teachings have inspired movements and individuals to tackle poverty in meaningful ways. From early Christian communities pooling resources to care for their members to modern social justice movements driven by religious convictions, the influence of biblical mythology is evident. In the Middle Ages, monasteries often served as centres of relief for the poor, providing food, shelter, and medical care. In more recent history, figures like Martin Luther King Jr. have drawn on biblical themes to advocate for systemic change, recognizing that poverty is not just a personal problem but a societal one.

Academic research supports the idea that poverty is not inevitable but often the result of structural issues, issues of inequality, lack of access to education, and systemic discrimination. Biblical mythology, when viewed through this lens, offers a framework for addressing these challenges. It calls for more than individual acts of kindness. It demands systemic change, rooted in a vision of justice where everyone has what they need to thrive. For example, the Jubilee year described in Leviticus was a radical idea for its time. Every fifty years, debts were to be forgiven, land returned to its original owners, and economic resets established to prevent generational poverty. While we might not implement such a system today in the same way, the principle remains relevant: societies must address the root causes of poverty, not just its symptoms.

Poverty is not merely an economic issue. It is a deeply human one, touching on questions of dignity, equity, and shared responsibility. Biblical mythology offers a rich source of wisdom for grappling with these questions. It challenges us to see poverty not as an abstract statistic but as a call to action, a reminder that the measure of any society is how it treats its most vulnerable members.

Pain And Suffering

In the context of eidotheosophy, understanding that bad things happen to good people is essential, and it's something that can be difficult to come to terms with. We tend to think that if we live right, if we follow the path of wisdom and virtue, we should be exempt from suffering, but that's simply not the case. Life is not always a direct reflection of one's actions or spiritual journey. Sometimes, bad things happen because of circumstances beyond our control. Someone might be the victim of a natural disaster, a crime, or an unjust system, despite their goodness and integrity. In these situations, there's no clear connection between the individual's actions and the misfortune they experience. It's a hard truth, but it's part of navigating the reality of life.

At times, suffering can be a result of the choices of others. This is where the concept of injustice comes in. Someone who has worked hard to live ethically might find themselves caught in the ripple effect of someone else's wrongdoings. It's a painful reminder that the actions of others have consequences, and often, those consequences don't just affect the wrongdoer; they affect everyone around them. The idea that bad things happen to good people because of someone else's choices challenges the notion of fairness, and yet, it's a very real part of the human experience.

There's also the fact that sometimes we experience suffering because of our own choices. This is where the consequences of our actions come into play. When we make poor decisions, when we act out of ignorance or selfishness, we set in motion a chain of events that can lead to negative outcomes. But even in these cases, the idea that suffering is always a direct result of our wrongdoings isn't always accurate. Life is messy, and people can make mistakes without those mistakes being catastrophic. And sometimes, we make decisions based on the best knowledge we have at the time, only to learn later that our choices weren't as wise as we thought.

Eidotheosophy doesn't provide a simple answer to why bad things happen to good people, but it does offer a way to approach suffering with wisdom. It encourages us to recognize that suffering is an inherent part of the human condition and not always something that can be avoided or neatly explained. Instead of looking at suffering as punishment or a sign of moral failure, it encourages us to approach it with a mindset that seeks understanding. Whether the suffering comes from external forces, the actions of others, or even our own mistakes, it's all part of the journey. It's not necessarily a reflection of our worth or the quality of our spiritual life.

The key is learning how to deal with suffering. In eidotheosophy, this involves seeking wisdom and understanding in the face of hardship, rather than simply blaming ourselves or others. It's about finding the deeper lessons in difficult times and using them to grow, even when we don't fully understand the reason for our pain. The idea is to approach suffering with the same reasoned and thoughtful approach that we apply to other aspects of life. It's not about avoiding pain or pretending it doesn't exist, but about finding a way to live through it, learn from it, and ultimately, let it shape us into better versions of ourselves.

Original Sin

In the context of eidotheosophy, the Christian doctrine of original sin is deeply problematic and harmful, especially when we look at its practical implications. The doctrine essentially tells people that the root cause of their misery, suffering, and moral failings is embedded in their inherent, unchangeable "sinfulness" as human beings. This view places the blame squarely on individuals, teaching them that their suffering is a consequence of their own flawed nature rather than a result of the societal systems and structures in which they live. The problem with this is that it shifts the focus away from the real issues in the world, issues such as unjust institutions, oppressive social systems, and unequal access to resources, that could potentially be changed through collective human effort. By focusing on the inherent sinfulness of humanity, the doctrine discourages people from looking at the social, political, and economic structures that perpetuate inequality, exploitation, and suffering.

When people internalize the idea that they are born sinful and that their misery is a direct consequence of that sinfulness, they are less likely to seek out solutions that address the external causes of their suffering. Instead, they might believe that their hardship is a result of their own moral failings or some divine punishment. This belief can lead to a sense of helplessness, where individuals feel powerless to change the conditions of their lives or the world around them. The idea of original sin works in tandem with the concept of predestination, where people are either doomed or saved by forces beyond their control. This makes it even harder for individuals to feel that they have agency in shaping their own lives or contributing to the betterment of society.

Eidotheosophy, on the other hand, encourages people to look beyond the idea of inherent sinfulness and to focus on the ways in which society and its institutions shape the experiences of individuals.

Instead of viewing personal suffering as a result of one's own sinful nature, eidotheosophy calls for a critical examination of the systems that perpetuate inequality, poverty, and injustice. It highlights the possibility of change, offering a more empowering framework for understanding the struggles of individuals and communities. Through collective social planning and action, these societal structures can be reformed to create a more just and equitable world.

The belief in original sin can have long-lasting effects on how people perceive themselves and their ability to contribute to societal change. If people believe that their suffering is inherent and unchangeable, they may feel resigned to their fate, unable to imagine a different reality. This mindset can lead to a sense of passivity, where individuals are less likely to take action to challenge the systems that are causing harm. By contrast, eidotheosophy challenges this notion and encourages a more active, engaged approach to both personal and collective transformation. It teaches that human beings are not inherently sinful but rather capable of growth, change, and improvement through reasoned understanding and collective action.

In practical terms, the doctrine of original sin has allowed oppressive systems to persist unchecked, as it diverts attention away from the real causes of human suffering. It creates an environment where individuals blame themselves for their struggles, instead of pointing to the institutional structures that perpetuate injustice. By focusing on personal sinfulness, it lets social and political systems off the hook, allowing them to continue operating in ways that benefit the few while exploiting the many. In this way, the doctrine has been used to justify the status quo and resist efforts for systemic change.

Ultimately, the harmful impact of the doctrine of original sin lies in its ability to shift the focus from collective responsibility to individual guilt. Eidotheosophy rejects this perspective and instead encourages a more constructive approach, where human beings are seen as capable of addressing societal issues through reason, compassion, and collective action. By acknowledging the external factors that contribute to human suffering and working together to change them, we can build a world that reflects the true potential of humanity, a world that is just, equitable, and free from the constraints of inherited guilt and shame.

Being Spiritual Vs. Being Religious

In the context of eidotheosophy, the difference between being spiritual and being religious lies in the way individuals approach their connection to the divine, the world around them, and their personal beliefs. Spirituality is often more personal, internal, and subjective. It's about seeking a deeper understanding of the self, the universe, and the divine, often without the need for formal structures or rituals. Spiritual individuals might engage with concepts like love, justice, or peace in a more fluid, open-ended way, looking for experiences or insights that resonate with their sense of purpose and existence. Spirituality is, in many ways, about personal experience and individual exploration, allowing people to define their own path to understanding what is sacred or meaningful.

On the other hand, being religious typically involves subscribing to a specific set of beliefs, practices, and doctrines within a recognized faith tradition. Religion often comes with defined rituals, moral codes, and community structures. It offers a framework for how people should live, worship, and relate to others and the divine. Religious individuals often follow established teachings and participate in communal rituals that reinforce their faith and identity within a broader community. Religion gives structure to belief, creating a collective identity and providing clear guidelines for moral and ethical behaviour based on sacred texts and traditions.

In the realm of eidotheosophy, this distinction is significant because it focuses on how people can integrate both faith and reason into their lives. The idea is not to strictly adhere to dogma but to find a way to explore divine wisdom through logical reasoning, personal reflection, and experiences. Eidotheosophy seeks to create a space where individuals can engage with both spiritual and religious aspects of their identity without being confined by rigid institutionalized structures. It allows for a fluid approach to spirituality, one that encourages people to seek divine wisdom and understanding, but in a way that also respects individual autonomy and critical thinking.

Spirituality in this context may be more about the individual's direct connection to the divine or their inner experiences, whereas religion could be seen as more of a collective understanding, where traditions and teachings are handed down through a community or institution. Eidotheosophy doesn't demand that one rejects religion outright but encourages a more thoughtful approach to how those religious ideas are understood and lived. It asks people to question, to think critically, and to engage with the concepts of faith in a way that respects both their personal spiritual journey and the wisdom of past religious traditions.

Being spiritual in this framework means prioritizing personal experience and reflection, while being religious implies following a structured system of beliefs and practices that are part of a broader, often communal, tradition. Eidotheosophy doesn't draw a strict line between the two but instead seeks to reconcile them, allowing room for personal interpretation while still honoring the importance of tradition and communal belief. Ultimately, the goal is to create a philosophy that supports individuals in navigating both their spiritual and religious experiences, without having to choose one over the other.

The Measure Of Faith

Eidotheosophy takes a grounded approach to the concept of faith, emphasizing that the measure of a person cannot and should not be tied to the measure of their faith. Faith, as an abstract and deeply personal experience, is not something that can be quantified or compared. Yet, throughout history and in many religious traditions, faith has often been used as a yardstick for spiritual worthiness. Eidotheosophy challenges this idea, reminding us that the value of a person lies in their actions, intentions, and humanity, not in the strength or consistency of their belief.

Struggling with faith is a universal part of the human experience. Many passages in biblical mythology reflect this reality. Figures like Job, who questioned god amidst immense suffering, or Thomas, who doubted the resurrection until he could see and touch evidence, serve as reminders that faith is not a straight line. It ebbs and flows, responding to the challenges, experiences, and emotions that define a person's life. The idea that faith might grow stronger or falter at different moments is not a failing but a natural reflection of our humanity. Eidotheosophy views this process as integral to spiritual growth, rather than as a measure of spiritual inadequacy.

The concept of justification by faith alone is another idea that eidotheosophy addresses with skepticism. Faith alone, without the substance of action, becomes an undefined measure. It cannot be tested or validated in any meaningful way. Biblical mythology itself provides examples that highlight the insufficiency of faith without deeds. James wrote that faith without works is dead, pointing to a practical and ethical dimension of belief. Actions, rather than abstract convictions, are what shape the world and leave a tangible impact on others. Faith might inspire those actions, but it is not a substitute for them.

Eidotheosophy asks us to question the logic of justification by faith alone. If faith is the determining factor for spiritual worthiness, how does one measure it? Is it the intensity of belief, the frequency of prayer, or the certainty of conviction? These are subjective and internal experiences that differ greatly from person to person. They cannot be observed, quantified, or judged by any standard. This makes the concept of justification by faith alone not only impractical but also exclusionary. It creates a hierarchy of believers, where those with unwavering faith are elevated above those who struggle or question. This does not align with the principles of fairness and inclusivity that eidotheosophy values.

Faith, in many ways, is a response to mystery and uncertainty. It is the willingness to believe in something greater than oneself, even when proof is absent. But in the context of eidotheosophy, faith is not a competition or a measure of superiority. A person who doubts or questions is no less valuable or worthy than one who believes without hesitation. In fact, the struggle with faith often leads to deeper understanding and more meaningful spiritual growth. Doubt pushes us to explore, learn, and engage with our beliefs in a way that blind certainty cannot.

The practical consequences of elevating faith as the sole measure of spiritual worth are also troubling. It creates a culture where doubt is stigmatized and questions are discouraged. People are taught to suppress their uncertainties rather than confront and explore them. This can lead to shallow or performative expressions of faith, where individuals say the right things but lack genuine engagement with their spirituality. It can also alienate those who struggle with belief, making them feel unworthy or excluded from spiritual communities.

Eidotheosophy promotes a more inclusive and compassionate understanding of faith. It recognizes that faith is deeply personal and sometimes fragile. It honours the journey of each individual, whether they are filled with certainty or grappling with doubt. Most importantly, it shifts the focus from the measure of one's faith to the measure of one's actions. How does a person treat others? Do they seek justice, show compassion, and contribute to the betterment of the world? These are the questions that matter, not the intensity or constancy of their belief.

Faith, as eidotheosophy sees it, is a tool rather than a test. It is a means to inspire and guide, not a benchmark for judgment. It is normal, even expected, for faith to waver. Life is unpredictable and challenging, and our beliefs often reflect that reality. By embracing the complexity of faith and rejecting the idea that it alone defines a person's worth, eidotheosophy offers a more reasonable and humane approach to spirituality.

Faith Is Not A Battlefield

One of the most liberating aspects of eidotheosophy is its complete rejection of the idea that faith must be a battlefield. There's no grand mission to convert others, no spiritual war over who's in or out, and no need to preach its principles to anyone unwilling to engage. The beauty of eidotheosophy lies in its deeply personal nature. It respects the idea that every spiritual journey is unique and shaped by an individual's experiences, questions, and search for meaning. Unlike many traditional religious systems that view proselytizing as an obligation, eidotheosophy finds value in a quieter, more introspective approach.

I have always been struck by how often organized religion paints the world in terms of us versus them. The saved versus the lost. The chosen versus the damned. The missionary zeal to win souls for a cause has often done more harm than good, creating division, distrust, and even outright violence. With eidotheosophy, there's no need for this. Faith is not a competition, and truth does not demand conquest. The idea of a spiritual army marching to subjugate others to its doctrine feels not only unnecessary but also completely counterproductive to the kind of spiritual growth that eidotheosophy encourages.

Eidotheosophy doesn't see belief as a fixed state. Faith is a process, one that evolves as we encounter new ideas, face new challenges, and grow in our understanding of ourselves and the world around us. Trying to impose this process on others makes no sense. What resonates for one person may not resonate for another. More importantly, spiritual understanding that is coerced or adopted out of fear rarely leads to meaningful transformation. Genuine belief has to come from a place of openness and curiosity, not from pressure or obligation.

This perspective is informed by both biblical mythology and historical context. In the early Christian tradition, there's a tension between Jesus' teachings about personal transformation and the institutional focus on spreading and enforcing doctrine that came later. Jesus, as depicted in biblical mythology, didn't seem particularly concerned with numbers or dominance. His focus was on individuals, on meeting people where they were and guiding them toward a better understanding of love, compassion, and justice. He didn't command his followers to build empires of belief; he simply invited them to live in a way that reflected divine wisdom.

History, on the other hand, shows us what happens when religion takes on the role of enforcer. Crusades, inquisitions, forced conversions, and cultural erasures; all justified in the name of saving souls. The irony is that these efforts often did the exact opposite of what they intended. Instead of drawing people closer to a higher truth, they alienated them from it. Instead of demonstrating the power of divine wisdom, they showed the corruption of human ambition. Eidotheosophy recognizes these patterns and refuses to replicate them. It chooses humility over conquest and understanding over domination.

What's fascinating about this approach is how freeing it is. Without the need to convert or convince others, believers can focus on their own journey. They can explore their questions and doubts without worrying about how their beliefs stack up against someone else's. This doesn't mean believers exist in isolation. There's still value in dialogue and community, but these interactions are about mutual growth rather than persuasion. Sharing ideas becomes an act of generosity, not a recruitment drive.

Eidotheosophy also takes into account the harm that can come from viewing others as projects or targets. When faith becomes about saving others, it often dehumanizes them in the process. People become souls to be won rather than individuals to be respected. This mindset can erode relationships and create an environment of judgment and superiority. Eidotheosophy rejects this entirely. It sees every person as valuable, not because they believe the right things, but simply because they are. This perspective fosters empathy and connection rather than division.

The absence of a mandate to preach also speaks to the broader philosophy of reason and logic that underpins eidotheosophy. Truth, if it's truly truth, doesn't need to be forced. It doesn't require campaigns or coercion. It simply exists, waiting to be discovered by those who are seeking it. In this way, eidotheosophy mirrors the natural world. Just as we don't need to convince people that gravity exists, we don't need to convince them of the principles of eidotheosophy. These principles stand on their own, evident in their alignment with both divine wisdom and real-world outcomes.

At its core, eidotheosophy is a deeply respectful philosophy. It respects the journey of the believer, the dignity of the nonbeliever, and the complexity of human understanding. It doesn't ask for allegiance or demand conformity. It simply invites reflection, offering tools to navigate the intersection of faith, reason, and life. This invitation is open to anyone, but it comes without strings. Those who choose to engage with it do so freely, not because they are pressured or frightened, but because they are ready to explore their own spiritual truth.

Rituals And Traditions

In eidotheosophy, the focus is on reason and practical understanding rather than the trappings of religion. Rituals and traditions are often seen as secondary to the essence of spiritual growth and ethical behaviour. That does not mean rituals and traditions are without value. They serve an important role for many people, offering emotional and spiritual benefits that cannot be overlooked. Eidotheosophy does not require the abandonment of these practices but instead suggests that their worth should be judged on their own merits.

Rituals and traditions can provide a sense of community and connection. Shared practices can create bonds that transcend individual experiences, grounding people in a sense of belonging. In biblical mythology, rituals like the Passover meal or the act of baptism served as collective expressions of faith and identity. These moments of shared practice can help believers feel connected to something greater than themselves, whether that is a divine presence, a cultural heritage, or a shared mission. The act of coming together to celebrate, mourn, or reflect can offer emotional solace and a sense of purpose.

For many, the physical acts of ritual, lighting a candle, singing a hymn, or kneeling in prayer, can create a meditative or reflective space that helps them focus their thoughts and emotions. These practices can become touchstones in the chaos of daily life, moments of grounding that allow people to reconnect with their values or their sense of the divine. In this way, rituals can hold deeply personal meaning that goes beyond any prescribed religious framework. They can serve as reminders of what is most important, whether that is gratitude, forgiveness, or hope.

While rituals and traditions have value, eidotheosophy encourages us to look critically at their role and purpose. It's important to distinguish between practices that enrich lives and those that impose harm. Traditions that perpetuate exclusion, inequality, or violence have no place in a reasoned approach to spirituality. Eidotheosophy would oppose practices that cause harm, whether that harm is physical, emotional, or social. The guiding principle here is simple: if a ritual or tradition brings peace, comfort, or understanding without causing harm, it can be seen as a positive element in someone's spiritual journey. However, if it creates division, fosters guilt, or enables abuse, it must be challenged and abandoned.

The idea that rituals and traditions should stand on their own merits also invites individuals to approach these practices with intention and reflection. Instead of participating out of obligation or fear, people can choose rituals that resonate with them personally. This makes the experience of ritual more authentic and meaningful. It allows for a diverse expression of spirituality, where people can adapt practices to fit their unique understanding and journey. This approach respects individuality while also acknowledging the shared human need for connection and meaning.

Rituals and traditions also carry cultural significance. They are often woven into the fabric of a community's identity, representing histories and values that have shaped generations. In biblical mythology, many rituals were deeply tied to the cultural and historical context of the people who practiced them. For instance, the Sabbath was not just a religious commandment but also a radical statement of human dignity and rest in a world dominated by labour and exploitation. These practices can hold lessons that transcend their original context, offering timeless insights into what it means to live a meaningful and ethical life.

Eidotheosophy does not dismiss the subjective value of rituals and traditions. It acknowledges that people find strength, peace, and inspiration in these practices. What matters is that these practices are chosen freely and embraced for the positive impact they have on individuals and communities. There is no obligation to adhere to rituals for their own sake, nor is there a need to discard them entirely.

Instead, the emphasis is on discernment, asking whether a practice contributes to personal or collective well-being.

By placing the evaluation of rituals and traditions in the hands of the individual, eidotheosophy promotes a sense of agency and responsibility. It encourages believers to engage with their spiritual practices thoughtfully and to consider how these practices align with their values and goals. This approach fosters a spirituality that is alive and dynamic, capable of adapting to new insights and circumstances while honouring the meaningful aspects of tradition.

Religion Vs. Science

The tensions between religion and science have been a source of conflict for centuries, with debates like the creation-evolution controversy, opposition to birth control, resistance to research on embryonic stem cells, and objections to medical advances like vaccinations, anaesthesia, and blood transfusions all illustrating the struggle. Many religious doctrines, particularly within Christianity, have historically pushed back against scientific discoveries or advancements that seem to challenge traditional beliefs or interpretations of biblical mythology. For example, the idea that life began through evolutionary processes rather than divine creation directly contradicts the literal interpretation of the creation story in Genesis. Similarly, when new medical technologies or scientific concepts emerge that were not even conceivable at the time the biblical texts were written, they are often met with skepticism or outright rejection from religious communities, who see them as a threat to their understanding of divine will.

In the context of eidotheosophy, this conflict should not exist. Eidotheosophy emphasizes a harmonious relationship between spiritual beliefs and scientific inquiry, suggesting that both can coexist without one undermining the other. The core of this philosophy is that spirituality is not about clinging to outdated interpretations of the world but rather about evolving with our understanding of the universe, which includes embracing scientific progress. There should be no inherent conflict between believing in a higher power and accepting scientific discoveries. If we understand the divine wisdom to be a living, dynamic force, then it would make sense that the universe itself is subject to ongoing exploration, discovery, and understanding. Science, in this view, is not opposed to spirituality but rather a tool that helps us uncover the intricacies of the world around us; an extension of our curiosity and reverence for the world we inhabit.

Eidotheosophy encourages us to see scientific knowledge as part of the divine gift of understanding, rather than something to be feared or dismissed. The knowledge gained through scientific inquiry, whether it's the theory of evolution, medical advancements, or breakthroughs in physics, should be seen as part of the greater picture of human progress and enlightenment. When new concepts or technologies emerge that were inconceivable in biblical times, we shouldn't force them into a framework that didn't have the language or concepts to understand them. Instead, we should allow for a flexible and evolving understanding of both our spiritual beliefs and our scientific knowledge. This approach invites us to adapt and grow, acknowledging that while biblical mythology provides valuable ethical guidance and a lens for understanding human nature, it was not written with the context of modern science in mind.

There are certain scientific concepts that simply couldn't have been imagined when biblical mythology was recorded. Quantum mechanics, the theory of relativity, genetic engineering; these are ideas that would have been entirely foreign to the writers of the scriptures. It is unreasonable to insist that our interpretation of the ancient texts must limit our understanding of these concepts today. By holding on too tightly to a rigid interpretation of scripture, we risk preventing ourselves from engaging with the progress we've made in science and medicine. Rather than seeing these developments as contrary to faith, we should view them as part of humanity's journey toward greater understanding and alignment with the divine. The very fact that humanity can continue to push the boundaries of knowledge and expand our understanding of the universe is something that should be celebrated, not feared.

Eidotheosophy offers a way to bridge this divide by suggesting that spiritual beliefs and scientific advancements can inform and enrich each other. When science uncovers a new truth, whether about the nature of the universe or the human body, it should be integrated into our understanding of the world in a way that aligns with the spiritual perspective. For example, if we discover that the process of evolution explains how life on Earth developed, we can still maintain a spiritual perspective that sees this as part of a larger divine plan. Science can help explain the "how" of existence, while spirituality can offer the "why," giving both a place in our broader understanding of life.

The rejection of scientific ideas or advancements, on the other hand, often stems from a fear that they might threaten the foundations of religious belief. But in the framework of eidotheosophy, there is no need for such fear. Religion and science can coexist if we view both as aspects of a larger quest for truth. Scientific progress doesn't negate the possibility of a divine plan; rather, it offers new insights into the intricacies of how that plan might unfold. Embracing this approach allows for a more open-minded, intellectually satisfying way of engaging with both faith and reason. It lets us move forward in our understanding of the world while still holding onto the spiritual values that guide us.

Colonialism

Addressing the effects of colonialism, both historical and ongoing, is a moral and spiritual necessity. Colonialism has left a deep scar on the world, disrupting societies, erasing cultures, and exploiting people and resources for the benefit of a privileged few. Its legacy continues to manifest in systemic inequalities, economic disparities, and the marginalization of Indigenous peoples and other communities. Eidotheosophy, with its focus on reason, justice, and the separation of divine wisdom from human agendas, calls on us to confront these realities with honesty and humility.

Colonialism, at its core, was an exercise in domination. European powers justified their conquests by claiming divine sanction, often citing biblical mythology as a moral foundation for their actions. They framed their invasions as missions to civilize and Christianize the so-called heathen world, presenting their cultural and religious norms as superior. This misuse of biblical mythology not only distorted its teachings but also caused immeasurable harm. Indigenous peoples were displaced, enslaved, and often killed. Their spiritual practices were demonized, their languages suppressed, and their histories rewritten to serve the colonizer's narrative.

Eidotheosophy urges us to reevaluate these justifications and their lingering effects. By separating the divine from human interpretations that served colonial agendas, we can begin to dismantle the ideologies that perpetuate inequality. Biblical mythology, when stripped of its colonial distortions, offers teachings of justice, compassion, and the inherent worth of every individual. These principles stand in direct opposition to the oppressive systems colonialism created and sustained.

The legacy of colonialism is not just a historical issue. It is alive in the systemic inequalities that persist today. Indigenous communities around the world face higher rates of poverty, lower access to education and healthcare, and ongoing struggles for land and sovereignty. The economic structures established during colonial times continue to benefit the descendants of colonizers at the expense of those who were colonized. These injustices demand action, not just acknowledgement.

Eidotheosophy emphasizes the importance of reasoned and evidence-based approaches to address these injustices. Repairing the damage of colonialism requires policies that promote equity, protect the rights of marginalized communities, and recognize the value of cultural diversity. It also requires a willingness to listen to those who have been most affected by colonial practices. Their voices, often silenced or ignored, must guide efforts toward reconciliation and healing.

One of the most harmful aspects of colonialism was its attack on cultural and spiritual identities. Many Indigenous spiritual practices were banned or stigmatized, replaced by imposed religious structures that did not reflect the beliefs or traditions of the people. This spiritual colonization was as damaging as the physical and economic exploitation, severing communities from their roots and their sense of self. Eidotheosophy calls for a recognition of the validity of diverse spiritual paths and an end to the idea that any one faith or culture holds a monopoly on truth. This perspective is not only more just but also more aligned with the principles of love and inclusion that should underpin faith.

Confronting the ongoing effects of colonialism also involves addressing the ways in which it has shaped our understanding of history and knowledge. Much of what is taught about colonialism centres the perspectives of the colonizers, framing their actions as inevitable progress rather than acknowledging the devastation they caused. This narrative perpetuates the invisibility of colonized peoples and their contributions. Reclaiming these stories and recognizing the resilience and resistance of Indigenous and other marginalized communities is a vital step toward justice.

Eidotheosophy rejects the idea that human systems of power and exploitation can be justified by divine will. It challenges us to see the harm colonialism has done and to take responsibility for dismantling its remnants. This involves not only recognizing the injustices of the past but also committing to creating a future where equity and respect are the norm. It calls on us to reject the ideologies of supremacy and dominance that underpinned colonialism and to embrace a worldview that values diversity and mutual respect.

The spiritual and practical work of confronting colonialism is not easy, but it is necessary. It requires us to question long-held beliefs, confront uncomfortable truths, and take action in ways that may challenge our own privileges. For those of us who are descendants of colonizers, it means acknowledging the benefits we have inherited from systems of oppression and working to dismantle them. For those who have been harmed by colonialism, it means reclaiming what was taken and demanding the justice and recognition long denied.

Dominionism

In the context of eidotheosophy, the rejection of dominionism is not just a political stance; it's a spiritual and ethical imperative. Dominionism, with its aim to impose a narrow interpretation of biblical law onto society, represents a profound misunderstanding of the relationship between faith, governance, and human freedom. At its core, dominionism is authoritarianism cloaked in religious language. It seeks to enforce a singular worldview, disregarding the diversity of beliefs, experiences, and values that make up a pluralistic society. This kind of coercion is incompatible with the principles of justice, compassion, and reason that eidotheosophy seeks to uphold.

The danger of dominionism lies in its insistence that one group's interpretation of biblical mythology should dictate the lives of everyone else. History provides ample evidence of the harm caused when religious ideology becomes the foundation for governance. From theocratic rule in the medieval era to more recent examples of oppressive regimes, the blending of religious authority with political power has often led to the suppression of dissent, the erosion of personal freedoms, and the persecution of minority groups. These outcomes stand in stark contrast to the teachings of love and inclusion found in the very texts dominionists claim to follow.

Eidotheosophy challenges the dominionist agenda by calling for a reasoned and ethical approach to faith. This perspective recognizes that the principles found in biblical mythology are best applied not through force or legislation, but through personal transformation and voluntary action. Faith, at its most meaningful, is a choice. It cannot be imposed without losing its essence. When Christians seek to dominate political systems to enforce their beliefs, they undermine the very message of Jesus, who taught through example, dialogue, and compassion rather than coercion.

Authoritarianism, whether religious or secular, poses a fundamental threat to human dignity and freedom. It thrives on control and conformity, stifling the diversity of thought and experience that drives progress and understanding. Religious authoritarianism, in particular, is insidious because it often claims divine endorsement for its actions, making dissent not just a political crime but a spiritual one. This conflation of political power and divine will leaves little room for dialogue or reform, creating a rigid system that resists accountability and perpetuates injustice.

The harm caused by dominionism extends beyond the immediate effects of its policies. By seeking to establish a government based on a single religious framework, dominionism alienates those who do not share the same faith or interpretation of biblical mythology. It fosters division and resentment, turning religion into a tool of exclusion rather than a source of connection. This goes against the very idea of community and shared humanity that faith should promote. It also risks turning people away from spirituality altogether, as they come to associate faith with oppression and intolerance.

Academic research and historical context both underscore the importance of separating religion and government. Secular governance, far from being an attack on faith, creates the conditions for genuine religious expression. It ensures that individuals are free to explore their beliefs without coercion or fear of reprisal. This freedom allows faith to flourish in its truest form, as a personal journey and a communal experience, rather than a tool of political control.

In opposing dominionism, eidotheosophy aligns itself with a broader commitment to justice and human rights. This commitment is not limited to the rejection of religious authoritarianism but extends to all forms of oppressive power. Whether it manifests as political tyranny, systemic inequality, or cultural dominance, authoritarianism denies people the agency and respect they deserve. It is the responsibility of every believer, guided by reason and compassion, to stand against these forces and work toward a society that honours the dignity and freedom of all.

The principles of eidotheosophy emphasize the importance of reasoning through faith, understanding its historical context, and applying its teachings in ways that uplift rather than oppress. By rejecting dominionism, we affirm that faith is not about controlling others but about striving to embody the values of love, justice, and humility. It is a reminder that true spiritual leadership seeks to serve rather than to dominate, to inspire rather than to enforce.

The Gospels And The Acts Of The Apostles

The formation of the Gospels and the Acts of the Apostles is one of the most fascinating aspects of biblical mythology. These texts weren't written in isolation or crafted as single, cohesive narratives from the start. They emerged over decades, shaped by oral traditions, the needs of early communities, and the perspectives of the authors themselves. Understanding how they came together helps illuminate the theological priorities, historical contexts, and human stories behind these foundational texts.

The Gospels, for example, are not eyewitness accounts in the strictest sense, nor are they straightforward biographies of Jesus. Instead, they are narratives that combine memory, theology, and storytelling. The earliest Gospel, Mark, was likely written around 70 CE. This was a turbulent time for the Jewish people, as the destruction of the Second Temple in Jerusalem had created a crisis of identity and faith. Mark's Gospel reflects a sense of urgency and focuses on the suffering of Jesus, portraying him as a figure who understands human pain and provides hope in the face of despair.

Matthew and Luke, written later, build on Mark's account while adding their unique perspectives. Matthew's Gospel leans heavily on Jewish traditions and scriptures, presenting Jesus as the fulfillment of Jewish prophecy. It was likely intended for a community that was grappling with its Jewish identity in a rapidly changing religious landscape. Luke, on the other hand, has a broader, more inclusive tone, emphasizing themes like compassion, social justice, and the inclusion of Gentiles. Luke's narrative is part of a two-volume work, the second part being the Acts of the Apostles, which provides a fascinating link between the life of Jesus and the growth of the early church.

John's Gospel is markedly different from the other three. Its language is more poetic, and its focus is more theological than historical. John's portrayal of Jesus emphasizes his divine nature and eternal significance. The Gospel of John may have been written to address specific theological debates within the early Christian community, such as the nature of Jesus and his relationship to god. These differences between the Gospels highlight the diversity of thought within early Christianity. They show us that these texts were not designed to provide a single, unified account but to address the needs and questions of different audiences.

The Acts of the Apostles shifts the focus from Jesus to his followers, tracing the spread of Christianity from Jerusalem to Rome. It is an ambitious narrative that showcases the transition from a small, localized movement to a global faith. The author of Luke-Acts, traditionally identified as Luke, provides a sweeping account of how the apostles, particularly Peter and Paul, carried the message of Jesus into the broader world. Acts explores themes like community, leadership, and the role of the Holy Spirit in guiding the church. It also highlights the tensions and challenges faced by early Christians, including persecution, internal divisions, and the struggle to define their identity in relation to Judaism and the Roman Empire.

The formation of these texts involved a complex interplay of oral tradition and written sources. Scholars believe that the authors of Matthew and Luke used not only Mark's Gospel as a source but also a now-lost collection of sayings known as Q. This shared material gives us insight into the teachings of Jesus that were considered most important by the early church. At the same time, the unique material in each Gospel shows how different communities remembered and interpreted Jesus' life and message. This process was not about creating historical records. It was about preserving the faith and making sense of it in light of the challenges and questions these communities faced.

The Acts of the Apostles also serves as a kind of theological roadmap, illustrating how the early church understood its mission and identity. The book begins in Jerusalem, with the apostles receiving the Holy Spirit at Pentecost, and ends in Rome, symbolizing the universal reach of the Christian message. Along the way, Acts highlights key moments of growth and conflict, such as the inclusion of Gentiles, the council of Jerusalem, and Paul's missionary journeys. These stories were meant to inspire and guide early Christians, showing them how to navigate their own challenges with faith and courage.

The formation of these texts was not a straightforward process. They were written in Greek, a language that many of Jesus' earliest followers probably did not speak fluently, and they reflect the cultural and political realities of the Greco-Roman world. They were also shaped by the theological debates of the time, as the early church worked to articulate its beliefs and distinguish itself from other religious movements. This context is crucial for understanding the Gospels and Acts not as static documents but as living texts that were deeply rooted in their historical moment.

What makes these texts so compelling is their ability to speak across centuries. They are both products of their time and timeless expressions of faith. By exploring their formation, we can see how biblical mythology is not just about preserving the past. It is about engaging with the present, asking questions, and seeking meaning. This process of formation reminds us that faith is not something handed down in a vacuum. It is something lived, questioned, and continually reimagined.

The Divine Teacher

Scholars largely agree that Jesus of Nazareth was a historical figure, a Jewish man from first-century Galilee whose life and teachings seem to have inspired the development of Christianity. What is less clear, and much more contested, is the nature of Jesus' identity as portrayed in Christian mythology. This distinction between the historical Jesus and the Christ of faith is essential for understanding how biblical mythology reflects and shapes religious belief. The Jesus of history refers to the man whose life is partially documented in historical records and oral traditions, while the Christ of faith embodies the theological and mythical figure central to Christianity. It is worth noting that there is no historical evidence to substantiate the existence of the Christ of faith beyond the religious texts and traditions that emerged after Jesus' death. Yet the power of this figure in shaping human history cannot be overstated.

In the context of eidotheosophy, the concept of the Christ of faith is seen to be the divine teacher. Whether this teacher existed as a historical reality or arose as a theological construct is less important than the ideas they represent. The Christ of faith becomes a symbol of god's influence, acting through what is often called the holy spirit, a term for the way through which divine wisdom is presented to humanity. The divine teacher in this sense is not bound to a single person or event but serves as a conduit for god's will, offering a model for living in alignment with divine principles.

What emerges from this perspective is a philosophy that centres on love, justice, and hope. These are not abstract ideals but practical guides for human relationships and societal organization. The teachings attributed to Jesus in biblical mythology emphasize radical love, a love that transcends boundaries of race, class, and even personal enmity. This love is not just emotional but deeply actionable, calling for acts of kindness, forgiveness, and sacrifice. In this way, the divine teacher is not just a preacher of morals but an exemplar of how to live them. The Sermon on the Mount, with its call to bless the poor, the meek, and the persecuted, provides a clear blueprint for a life steeped in empathy and justice.

Justice is another cornerstone of the divine teacher's philosophy. Biblical mythology portrays Jesus as someone who challenged the status quo, critiquing systems of power and advocating for those marginalized by society. He stood against corruption among religious leaders, condemned exploitation, and championed the dignity of every human being. These actions resonate strongly in the context of eidotheosophy, which seeks to sift divine wisdom from human distortion. Justice, as modelled by the divine teacher, is not merely a legal principle but a sacred duty to protect and uplift the vulnerable. It is a reminder that the fight for fairness and equality is not just a societal task but a spiritual one.

Hope ties these principles together, offering a vision of a better world not just in some distant afterlife but here and now. Biblical mythology frames the divine teacher as someone who believed in transformation, not just the transformation of individuals but of entire communities. This hope is not naive; it recognizes suffering and injustice but insists that they are not the final word. Hope challenges believers to see the world as it could be, not just as it is, and to work tirelessly to bridge that gap. This is where the philosophy of the divine teacher transcends its religious origins, becoming a universal call to action.

In reevaluating the Christ of faith through the lens of eidotheosophy, we find a profound synthesis of spirituality and practicality. The divine teacher does not demand blind faith or rigid adherence to doctrine but invites a thoughtful, active engagement with the world. This approach recognizes that divine wisdom is not static; it evolves as humanity learns and grows. The divine teacher's philosophy of love, justice, and hope becomes a guide not just for personal transformation but for collective progress. It challenges us to ask how we might live more meaningfully, care more deeply, and build a world that reflects the best of god's wisdom.

The term "pseudepigrapha" refers to a collection of ancient writings that are often attributed to biblical figures or prophets but were not actually written by them. The word itself means "false writings," which is fitting because these texts were deliberately associated with well-known biblical personalities to give them more authority. The authors of these texts weren't trying to mislead people in a malicious way necessarily, but they were using the names of revered figures to lend weight to their ideas and teachings. These works often address important religious, philosophical, or theological topics, but they were written centuries after the figures they claim to represent had lived.

When we look at the pseudepigrapha, it's clear that these writings were deeply connected to the religious and cultural context of the time. Many of them emerged during the Second Temple period, a time when Judaism was undergoing significant changes. This period saw the rise of new religious ideas, many of which were influenced by Greek philosophy, Hellenistic culture, and the political struggles between the Jewish people and foreign rulers. The pseudepigrapha often reflect these influences and offer insights into how people were trying to make sense of their faith and identity in a time of upheaval. By attributing their work to figures like Enoch, Moses, or even Isaiah, the authors were trying to ground these new ideas in an authoritative tradition that people could trust.

A key aspect of understanding the pseudepigrapha is recognizing the role that literary tradition played in the ancient world. In many ancient cultures, it was common for writers to use the names of famous figures to authenticate their works. The idea of authorship in the modern sense didn't exist in the same way it does today. Instead of focusing on who wrote a text, the emphasis was on the content and the message it conveyed. In this context, pseudepigrapha were not seen as dishonest forgeries but rather as attempts to continue and expand on the religious traditions of the past. The authors were not inventing new doctrines or ideas, but rather interpreting and building upon the ones they inherited, trying to offer fresh perspectives for their time.

Some of the most well-known pseudepigraphal works include the Book of Enoch, the Apocalypse of Baruch, and the Assumption of Moses. These writings cover a wide range of topics, from apocalyptic visions to moral teachings. The Book of Enoch, for example, is particularly significant because it delves into the realm of angels, fallen angels, and the cosmic order. This book was highly influential in certain Jewish sects, especially the Essenes, and it even made its way into early Christian thought. However, because it was not included in the Hebrew Bible or the Christian New Testament, it is often regarded as outside the canon. The ideas contained in the Book of Enoch were considered valuable and spiritually enriching by some groups but not universally accepted as authoritative.

The presence of pseudepigrapha in the religious landscape also raises important questions about the formation of the biblical canon. The canon, as we know it today, was not decided upon until centuries after the texts were written. The process of determining which books would be considered sacred and authoritative involved a great deal of debate and disagreement. Some of the writings that were excluded from biblical mythology, were highly influential in the development of early Christian and Jewish thought, yet they were ultimately deemed non-canonical. This exclusion wasn't necessarily about rejecting the value of these texts; rather, it was about maintaining a certain coherence and unity within the tradition that became biblical mythology.

It's also important to note that pseudepigrapha were not unique to Jewish or Christian traditions. In many ancient cultures, the use of attributed authorship appears to be somewhat common. The Greeks, Romans, and Egyptians also had a history of producing texts attributed to famous historical or mythological figures. In some cases, these works were intended as a form of political propaganda, in others as a way to preserve or revitalize cultural traditions. This practice speaks to a broader human tendency to connect new ideas with respected figures from the past. By doing so, these new works gained a sense of legitimacy and a place in the cultural conversation.

When considering the pseudepigrapha in the context of the biblical mythology, it's important to approach them with an understanding of their historical and cultural significance. These works were products of their time, reflecting the concerns, beliefs, and aspirations of the people who wrote them. They were not written in isolation but as part of a larger religious and philosophical dialogue. Many did not make it into official canon, but such pseudepigrapha provides valuable insights into the religious climate of the time and the ways in which people were grappling with the big questions about god, the cosmos, and humanity's place in the world.

In the broader context of biblical interpretation, the pseudepigrapha challenge us to think critically about the nature of scripture and authority. These texts remind us that the development of religious traditions is not a simple, linear process. Rather, it's a complex and ongoing conversation in which new ideas are constantly being debated, refined, and incorporated into the broader tradition. The pseudepigrapha, like other biblical writings, represent voices that were part of that conversation, even if they were not ultimately included in the canonical version of biblical mythology. Their inclusion or exclusion from the canon doesn't necessarily determine their value or relevance; it simply reflects the choices made by the communities that shaped the biblical tradition over time.

Ephesians

The Book of Ephesians has long been a subject of interest for those studying early Christian writings. It stands as one of the letters in the New Testament that carries a distinctive tone, especially when it comes to the language used in regard to relationships, salvation, and the community of believers. While it is often seen as a letter of encouragement and spiritual guidance, there are sections within Ephesians that raise questions about how its words were meant to be understood, particularly concerning the potential for divisiveness. The letter is frequently attributed to Paul, but its authorship and historical context are matters of debate among scholars. Some believe it was written by Paul, while others argue it was written later by one of his followers, in a time when the early Christian communities were beginning to expand and take shape more distinctly from Jewish traditions.

Ephesians is known for its teachings about unity within the body of Christ, but some of its language can also be read as deeply exclusive. The letter speaks often about the separation between Jews and Gentiles, creating a framework of inclusion and exclusion that could be interpreted in ways that divide people. The passage in Ephesians 2, for instance, speaks about how Christ has broken down the wall of hostility between Jews and Gentiles. While this could be seen as a positive declaration of unity, the emphasis on the prior division can also create a sense of "us versus them." The language of division and distinction between different groups may have been understood as more conciliatory in its time, trying to reconcile two groups that had historically been at odds. However, in a modern context, the emphasis on these divisions could easily be misunderstood as reinforcing lines between different groups of people rather than calling for true unity and shared identity.

The passage is powerful in that it highlights the transformation that was seen as necessary for the establishment of a new, unified Christian identity. But the underlying implication of who belongs and who is "outside" could, if taken too literally, contribute to a mindset that fosters exclusion. The early Christian community was, after all, grappling with how to bring together various traditions, cultures, and religious practices. The tension between those who were rooted in Jewish customs and those who came from Gentile backgrounds was significant. Ephesians presents the resolution to this conflict through the reconciling work of Christ, but there is a subtle undertone of recognizing and addressing the differences between the groups before they could be unified.

In other parts of the letter, Ephesians uses language that can be seen as asserting an authority over other systems or ways of thinking. The writer speaks in strong terms about the need to "put off" the old self and "put on" the new self in Christ, which could create a sense of sharp distinction between those who have accepted Christ and those who have not. The language of transformation and renewal, while certainly part of the Christian message, is expressed in ways that could be interpreted as a critique or rejection of non-believers or those who still cling to older religious systems. In a way, the letter points to a kind of spiritual superiority, implying that those who have embraced Christ's message are somehow above those who haven't.

This theme can be particularly divisive when viewed through the lens of how religious communities tend to interact with the outside world. While Ephesians calls for unity among believers, the tone of exclusivity regarding non-believers or those outside the fold could contribute to a sense of spiritual elitism. The letter suggests that salvation and the new identity found in Christ are not just individual choices, but markers of a distinct community that has been set apart from the world. In this way, the language of Ephesians could be seen as potentially creating spiritual divisions rather than fostering a truly inclusive, global community of believers.

When you combine this with the broader historical context of the time, the situation becomes more complex. The early Christian movement was emerging from a Jewish tradition that had long seen itself as the "chosen" people, and the conflict between Jewish and Gentile Christians was one of the defining issues in the first century. As the letter of Ephesians was being written, the distinction between these two groups still loomed large. The language in Ephesians may have been designed to address this tension, seeking to affirm the unity of believers while also acknowledging their previous differences. But these differences, when highlighted too strongly, could easily be seen as a justification for division rather than reconciliation.

Looking at the letter through the lens of biblical mythology, the story that Ephesians tells about Christ breaking down barriers and bringing unity takes on a more nuanced meaning. It's not just about breaking down a wall between Jews and Gentiles; it's about the potential danger of creating new divisions in the name of religious transformation. The language of salvation and unity can easily become a tool for creating boundaries, and when this idea is extended to the way the Christian faith is lived out today, it can lead to divisions within communities of faith. If the language of Ephesians is interpreted as reinforcing the idea of a hierarchical, exclusive community, it could foster conflict, even as it calls for peace.

One of the challenges with Ephesians and its potentially divisive language is how it has been interpreted and used throughout history. For centuries, certain passages in the letter have been invoked to justify exclusionary practices or to maintain distinctions between groups within the Christian world. The letter has been used to support ideas of doctrinal purity, church hierarchy, and even the rejection of other religious traditions. The language of exclusivity found in Ephesians has sometimes been used as a means to assert power over others, rather than focusing on the message of reconciliation and unity that is also central to the letter.

In examining the language of Ephesians, it's essential to remember that the historical context played a key role in shaping its content. The author was addressing specific issues facing the early Christian community, particularly the tension between Jewish and Gentile believers. What might have been seen as a call for unity in the first century may, when read through a modern lens, feel more like an assertion of religious superiority. It's important to read Ephesians with an understanding of both the historical and theological context, recognizing the challenges of uniting diverse groups under a common faith. The letter's language might have served to address a deep internal conflict in early Christianity, but it also has the potential to perpetuate the very divisions it sought to overcome. The challenge, then, is to reclaim the message of unity and reconciliation while being mindful of how the language of exclusivity can lead to unnecessary divisions.

The letter to the Colossians is one of those writings that stands out in the New Testament for its blend of practical advice and deep theological reflections. At first glance, it seems like a pretty straightforward letter from Paul, offering encouragement and instruction to the Christian community in Colossae. However, there are aspects of this letter that raise some important questions, particularly when viewed through the lens of pseudepigrapha. The letter to the Colossians, like some other New Testament epistles, has been the subject of debate about whether it was truly written by Paul or by one of his followers in his name. These questions about authorship matter because they affect how we understand the messages and intentions behind the letter, especially as it contains themes that, in some ways, seem inconsistent with the broader letters of Paul.

Colossians is a letter that, at its core, deals with both theological ideas and everyday matters for the early Christian community. It addresses the nature of Christ and the sufficiency of his work, urging the believers to hold firm to the truth of the gospel and not to be swayed by false teachings. It also gets into more practical areas, offering advice on relationships, work, and how Christians should live in light of their new identity in Christ. But while these themes sound familiar, there are some passages that have caused concern. For one, the letter seems to lay out a more hierarchical view of the Christian community than we might expect from Paul's other writings. The instructions for wives, husbands, children, and slaves have raised eyebrows, especially in modern discussions about equality and human dignity.

The theological claims made in Colossians are also worth noting. It emphasizes the preeminence of Christ, asserting that he is the image of the invisible god and the head of the church. This fits neatly within the broader Christian narrative of Christ's divinity and his central role in salvation. However, the way the letter handles the relationship between

Christ and the church seems to elevate Christ in ways that go beyond what we see in the earlier parts of the New Testament. The letter is filled with grandiose language about Christ's supremacy, yet the focus on his cosmic role can also feel a bit disconnected from the practical struggles and experiences of the early Christian communities. It's almost as though Colossians is trying to draw a sharp line between the heavenly, divine Christ and the earthly, human realities of life – which seems to be a somewhat different emphasis than what we find in, say, the gospels or Paul's earlier letters.

One of the more striking elements of Colossians is its warning against false teachings, specifically the influence of what seems to be a mix of Jewish and Gentile religious traditions. The letter urges the Colossians not to be taken captive by philosophy or empty deceit, and it warns against human traditions, legalistic observances, and the worship of angels. While these warnings are valid in the context of the early church, they also seem to be somewhat inconsistent with the larger New Testament picture of freedom in Christ. There's a tension here between a message of freedom from the law and the push to avoid certain "higher" spiritual practices that seem to come from a similar religious context. The language of the letter, at times, seems to promote an almost gnostic-style spirituality, where special knowledge and spiritual rituals are considered essential for maintaining a true relationship with Christ. This emphasis on a more mystical and esoteric form of faith doesn't fully align with the broader teachings found elsewhere in the New Testament, leading some to question whether the letter accurately represents Paul's teachings or if it reflects later theological developments.

Another concern is the practical advice given in Colossians, particularly regarding the roles of wives, husbands, children, and slaves. In a world where many people look to biblical teachings for guidance on relationships and family dynamics, the letter's instructions can seem problematic. Wives are instructed to submit to their husbands, and slaves are told to obey their masters. These directives seem to reinforce traditional hierarchies that are troubling when viewed through the lens of modern concepts of equality and justice. Some scholars argue that these teachings are culturally conditioned, reflecting the social norms of the time, but it's hard to ignore the fact that they've been used throughout history to justify the subjugation of women and the oppression of slaves. When we consider the possibility that Colossians wasn't written directly by Paul, these themes take on an even more complex light. Could the letter reflect a more conservative, hierarchical view of society that developed after Paul's time, rather than Paul's own progressive vision for the church?

There's also the issue of Colossians' call to avoid "empty deceit" and "worldly wisdom," which seems to stand in contrast to the more open and reasoned discussions we see in other parts of the New Testament, especially in Paul's letters to the Corinthians and Romans. Paul is often seen as someone who encourages believers to engage with the world around them, to challenge their thinking, and to be transformed by the renewing of their minds. In Colossians, however, there's a sense that believers should avoid certain forms of thinking and worldly knowledge altogether. The letter suggests that the Colossians already have everything they need in Christ, which, on one hand, is a reassuring message, but on the other hand, it risks creating an attitude of isolationism and intellectual stagnation. When you start to draw lines between "worldly" knowledge and "divine" wisdom in this way, it can create an unhealthy fear of intellectual exploration and a closed-off attitude toward new ideas.

When we think about Colossians in the context of pseudepigrapha, these concerns become even more pronounced. If the letter wasn't actually written by Paul but by someone else claiming his authority, it could reflect a later stage in the development of Christian thought. In the years following Paul's ministry, the early Christian church was working through a number of theological and social issues.

Colossians could represent a more developed and, perhaps, more exclusive vision of Christianity; one that sought to establish clear boundaries against external philosophies and religious practices. This letter, while offering wisdom in many ways, might also be a reflection of the struggles of a church that was grappling with how to maintain its identity in a world filled with competing beliefs. In this light, Colossians might serve as an example of how the early Christian movement wrestled with its relationship to the surrounding cultures, and how later writers might have overemphasized the need for separation from those cultures in ways that don't always align with the more inclusive messages of earlier Christian teachings.

The letter to the Thessalonians has been a subject of considerable debate, particularly the second letter, which has raised concerns about its authenticity and its message. While the first letter to the Thessalonians is widely accepted as genuinely written by Paul, the second one introduces themes that don't align quite so neatly with his other writings, and some of its teachings even contradict aspects of biblical scripture. One of the biggest issues with 2 Thessalonians is the way it handles the theme of the "day of the Lord," which Paul addresses in a very different tone and manner in his other letters. The way 2 Thessalonians speaks about the end times and the return of Christ seems to have taken a more rigid and dogmatic stance that doesn't fit with Paul's earlier, more flexible teachings on the subject.

In 2 Thessalonians, the idea of the day of the Lord is presented with an almost apocalyptic sense of finality. It describes a time when a great rebellion will occur, and a man of lawlessness will rise to deceive many, leading them into destruction. This echoes themes we see in other apocalyptic writings, particularly in the Hebrew scriptures and in the later parts of the New Testament, but it comes across as almost a warning in a way that seems inconsistent with Paul's more hopeful and redemptive tone elsewhere. The focus is much more on the destruction and punishment of the wicked, which doesn't feel in line with Paul's earlier emphasis on mercy, grace, and reconciliation. His letters, particularly those to the Corinthians and Romans, stress the idea that god is not willing that any should perish, but that all should come to repentance. The tone in 2 Thessalonians, however, seems much more focused on the impending judgment of those who refuse to believe. It's almost as if the letter is drawing a hard line between the faithful and the unrighteous, which contradicts Paul's overall message of god's inclusive love and patience.

Then, there's the issue of the "man of lawlessness," who is presented in 2 Thessalonians as a clear sign of the end times. This figure is described as someone who opposes all that is called god and exalts himself above every so-called god or object of worship. While this could be seen as a reference to a future political or religious leader, the language used in 2 Thessalonians seems to borrow heavily from other apocalyptic literature, such as the Book of Daniel and the writings in Revelation, which raises questions about whether this was actually Paul's voice or the voice of a later writer. Paul's writings tend to focus more on personal transformation and the church's mission in the world rather than creating a detailed eschatological framework. The depiction of this "man of lawlessness" doesn't fit neatly with his usual style, and it feels somewhat out of place when we think about the broader themes of grace and redemption that Paul typically emphasizes.

Another aspect of 2 Thessalonians that stands out is its insistence on the idea that the Thessalonians should not be easily swayed by false teachings or rumours about the return of Christ. It sounds reasonable enough on the surface, but the way it's framed seems to suggest a level of paranoia about deception that doesn't appear in Paul's earlier letters. There's a sense of urgency in 2 Thessalonians, a fear that believers might be led astray by someone claiming to know the times and the seasons of Christ's return. While Paul certainly cautioned against false prophets and teachings in his other letters, the tone in 2 Thessalonians feels much more intense and even dismissive of anyone who tries to predict the end times. It's almost as if the letter is telling people to shut down any conversation about the return of Christ that isn't strictly in line with the author's understanding, which is not how Paul typically approached these matters. Paul generally encouraged believers to remain watchful and hopeful, but without becoming obsessed with dates and predictions.

There's also the issue of the way the letter deals with idleness and work. In 2 Thessalonians, the writer addresses a problem in the

Thessalonian church where some people had become idle, waiting for the day of the Lord, and were not contributing to the community's work. While this message aligns with Paul's broader teaching that believers should continue to work and contribute to society, there's a harsher tone in 2 Thessalonians that doesn't seem to fit with his usual encouragement. The letter tells the Thessalonians to avoid anyone who is not willing to work and to discipline those who are idle. This may seem straightforward, but the language used is more extreme than what we see in Paul's earlier letters, where he is more focused on encouraging the church to help and support one another. The approach in 2 Thessalonians is much more about exclusion and condemnation, which feels somewhat disconnected from Paul's message of love and unity in Christ.

All of these issues raise significant questions about the authorship and the message of 2 Thessalonians. If we consider the possibility that this letter was not actually written by Paul, but by someone who wanted to carry on his teachings in a particular direction, these inconsistencies make more sense. A later writer might have been influenced by the apocalyptic and judgment-focused writings of the time, like those of the Hebrew prophets or the emerging Christian tradition, and felt the need to take a harder stance on issues like the return of Christ, work, and the role of false teachers. These elements seem to reflect a different stage in the development of Christian thought, one that places more emphasis on strict rules, boundaries, and expectations.

The tension between 2 Thessalonians and the rest of the New Testament is hard to ignore. When we consider its themes of judgment, apocalyptic fear, and exclusion, it's difficult to reconcile these messages with the inclusive love and grace that is so central to the teachings of Jesus and Paul's letters. If 2 Thessalonians was indeed written by someone else, it could represent a shift in the early Christian movement, one that became more concerned with protecting the church from outside influences and preserving a sense of orthodoxy. The letter's message, while still valuable in its own way, raises important questions about how the early church was grappling with issues of identity, authority, and the future, and whether those concerns were always in line with the teachings of the apostles.

1 Timothy, one of the pastoral epistles, has been the subject of much debate, particularly because of certain themes and instructions that some see as problematic or contrary to the broader messages found in biblical scripture. There are passages in this letter that seem to contradict the teachings of Jesus and the spirit of grace that runs throughout Paul's other letters. One of the biggest concerns is the way 1 Timothy handles the role of women in the church. It's a theme that continues to spark division and confusion. The letter includes strong instructions about women being silent in church and not having authority over men. This has raised eyebrows for centuries because it seems to contradict the teachings of Paul in places like Galatians, where he speaks about there being neither male nor female in Christ. The sharp distinction made in 1 Timothy between men and women, especially in relation to leadership, feels at odds with the more egalitarian sentiment expressed elsewhere in the New Testament.

In 1 Timothy, Paul instructs that women should learn in silence and submission, and he places restrictions on their role in the church, which raises the question: did Paul really believe that women should be subservient in all things, or is this a later insertion? Some scholars argue that these verses were added after Paul's time, possibly as a response to cultural pressures or emerging church structures that sought to enforce male dominance. If we consider the broader context of early Christian communities, we see that women played significant roles in ministry. Phoebe, a deacon, Priscilla, a teacher, and Junia, an apostle, are all examples of women who were recognized in leadership roles in the early church. Given this, it's hard to reconcile these specific instructions in 1 Timothy with the more inclusive teachings about leadership and gifts that we see elsewhere in the New Testament.

Another troubling aspect of 1 Timothy is the harsh language it uses regarding false teachings. The letter warns against false teachers who, it is said, will teach "doctrines of demons" and lead people astray. This language, while perhaps intended to emphasize the seriousness of deviating from the truth, can come across as overly divisive and dismissive. It suggests that those who disagree with the author's views are not just wrong but actively promoting evil. This tone seems to contradict the spirit of love, patience, and dialogue that we see in other parts of the New Testament, especially in Paul's letters, where he encourages believers to gently correct one another and work toward unity. The warning in 1 Timothy about false teachers feels more severe and less tolerant, perhaps reflecting the challenges the early church faced in maintaining doctrinal purity, but it doesn't always sit well with the more open and redemptive spirit of the gospel.

Additionally, the way 1 Timothy addresses the issue of wealth is another point of contention. It contains warnings about the dangers of money and the love of wealth, which is consistent with Jesus' teaching in the Gospels. However, 1 Timothy also seems to create a sharp division between the rich and the poor in a way that seems contrary to the gospel message of inclusivity. The letter advises that the rich should not place their hope in their wealth, but the way it frames the issue makes it feel like the wealthy are inherently at fault for their riches. While it's true that the love of money can lead to many problems, there is also a recognition throughout the New Testament that wealth itself is not evil, but the way it is used or worshipped can be. Paul's letters, in particular, speak of the potential for the wealthy to use their resources for good, to share, and to support the community. 1 Timothy, however, takes a much more cautionary and even condemning approach, which raises questions about whether this perspective truly reflects the heart of the gospel or if it represents an overly harsh stance on wealth that was perhaps influenced by the cultural attitudes of the time.

Finally, 1 Timothy includes instructions on the qualifications for church leaders, particularly overseers and deacons. These qualifications are often seen as very rigid and, in some cases, unrealistic. The emphasis on moral perfection and personal character may have been meant to establish high standards for leaders, but it's also problematic because it implies that only those who are without fault are qualified to serve in these roles. The qualification of being "above reproach" is one that seems particularly difficult to measure and could potentially lead to exclusion of those who might be spiritually mature but fall short in certain areas. It's also important to remember that early Christian communities were not perfect, and the leaders were often chosen not because of their perfection but because of their willingness to serve and their deep commitment to the teachings of Jesus. In this way, the qualifications listed in 1 Timothy might be seen as an overemphasis on external behaviours rather than on the internal transformation and heart for ministry that should guide leadership.

All of these themes in 1 Timothy raise significant questions about its authorship and the context in which it was written. Many scholars argue that 1 Timothy, along with 2 Timothy and Titus, was not actually written by Paul but by someone in his name, perhaps to maintain authority or to respond to emerging issues in the early church. The letter's instructions on women, false teachers, wealth, and leadership seem to reflect a particular perspective that may have developed later, as the church became more institutionalized and concerned with maintaining order and authority. If we consider the possibility that 1 Timothy was written by someone else, the inconsistencies between this letter and Paul's other writings make more sense. It could be that the letter was meant to address specific concerns of a later time, and as such, its teachings may not fully align with the broader message of the New Testament.

Ultimately, 1 Timothy serves as a reminder that the New Testament is not a single, unified voice but a collection of writings from different perspectives and communities, each grappling with the challenges of faith and practice. Some of the teachings in 1 Timothy might seem out of place or even contradictory to other parts of scripture, but that doesn't necessarily mean they are invalid. It simply means we need to approach these writings with discernment, considering the historical context and the broader themes of love, grace, and inclusion that run through biblical mythology. The key is to understand that not everything attributed to Paul or the early church should be taken as absolute, and that we must continually evaluate and reinterpret scripture in light of the overarching message of the gospel.

2 Timothy, like the other pastoral epistles, has been the subject of scrutiny for various reasons. Some of the themes and writings within this letter raise concerns, especially when compared to the broader teachings of the New Testament. A lot of the issues arise when we consider the message of grace and love that runs throughout the gospels and Paul's earlier letters. While 2 Timothy is often seen as a deeply personal letter, intended to encourage Timothy and remind him of the importance of remaining faithful, certain passages seem to carry a tone that contradicts the openhearted, inclusive nature of the gospel.

One of the primary concerns with 2 Timothy is its tone regarding suffering and the role of hardship in the Christian life. There are repeated mentions of enduring hardship and suffering for the gospel's sake, which, on one level, is consistent with what Jesus taught about taking up one's cross. But in 2 Timothy, the way suffering is framed can seem more like a test of one's loyalty to the church or the doctrine rather than a reflection of the love and self-sacrifice that Jesus modelled. Paul talks about his own imprisonment and encourages Timothy to "share in suffering" as a good soldier of Christ Jesus. This could be interpreted as an overemphasis on suffering as proof of faith, suggesting that only those who endure hardship are truly following the path of Christ. This stance can be problematic because it risks elevating suffering to a level where it becomes an unnecessary burden, rather than something that can be transformative or a tool for spiritual growth.

Another concerning theme in 2 Timothy is the warning against "godless chatter" and "opponents of the truth." The letter suggests that those who oppose the gospel are not just misguided but actively working against god's will. While it's important to address false teachings, this kind of language seems to paint anyone who disagrees with a particular interpretation of the faith as an enemy. There's a clear sense of division in this letter, and it seems to encourage a combative attitude toward others, especially those with differing views. This can be troubling because it doesn't align with the more compassionate and loving tone found in much of Jesus' ministry, where he encouraged his followers to love their enemies and pray for those who persecuted them. The idea of labelling those who disagree with certain doctrinal points as adversaries could lead to an unhealthy and divisive spirit in the church, which has often led to conflict rather than understanding.

2 Timothy also has passages that talk about "rightly dividing the word of truth" and avoiding "worldly and empty chatter." While the call to handle scripture carefully and wisely is understandable, this could be seen as a form of gatekeeping. The emphasis on the purity of doctrine and correct interpretation of scripture might discourage open, honest dialogue about different perspectives. It also seems to put the focus on the intellectual and doctrinal aspects of faith rather than the relational and transformative elements. If scripture is used primarily as a tool for defending a specific doctrinal position or for creating barriers between people, it loses the life-giving, inclusive power that it's supposed to have. The way 2 Timothy stresses the importance of "rightly dividing" could be seen as discouraging the free exploration of ideas and experiences that can enrich one's understanding of the faith.

Another theme in 2 Timothy that raises concerns is its apparent view of the last days and the way it portrays people who are not aligned with the church. Paul talks about how people in the "last days" will be "lovers of self" and "lovers of money," "ungrateful," "unholy," and so on. While these traits might seem to fit the description of a society that is falling away from faith, this kind of language can easily slip into judgmentalism. It creates a sharp us-versus-them dichotomy, suggesting that those outside the faith are hopelessly lost and deserving of condemnation. This portrayal of the "last days" can lead to fear-mongering and anxiety about the state of the world, as well as a tendency to view outsiders as irredeemable. This runs counter to the inclusive message of the gospel, which calls for outreach and reconciliation, rather than division and condemnation.

There is also a specific focus on church leadership in 2 Timothy, which emphasizes the importance of teaching and passing on sound doctrine. This is important, but the way the letter frames this could be problematic. It sets up an almost idealized vision of church leadership, where the focus is on maintaining doctrinal purity and upholding tradition, even at the expense of other priorities. While maintaining sound doctrine is undoubtedly important, the letter's approach may risk elevating the role of leadership to an almost authoritarian level, where the leaders' interpretation of scripture becomes unquestionable. This can lead to a hierarchical structure that stifles discussion, creativity, and the freedom to wrestle with faith. It may also encourage a culture where questioning or seeking alternatives is seen as a threat to the integrity of the church.

Finally, 2 Timothy is often seen as addressing the perceived abandonment of the faith by certain individuals, and the letter includes strong language about avoiding such people. The idea of "fleeing from youthful passions" and "avoiding those who cause division" could be seen as a way of drawing clear lines between the faithful and those who are not. While it's true that some behaviours and attitudes need to be avoided, the way this letter stresses avoidance can feel unwelcoming. It creates an "in-group" and "out-group" mentality, rather than encouraging reconciliation or understanding. This kind of exclusive mindset doesn't fit well with the message of Jesus, who spent much of his time with those on the margins, seeking to bring them in rather than push them away.

When we read 2 Timothy with these themes in mind, it becomes clear that this letter is more concerned with the preservation of church tradition and the defence of doctrinal purity than with embodying the love and compassion that Jesus showed. While some of the teachings in 2 Timothy are undoubtedly rooted in a desire to protect the early church from false teachings and outside influences, the tone and approach can feel overly harsh and divisive. It's important to remember that this letter, like other parts of the New Testament, must be read in light of the broader message of the gospel, which is one of reconciliation, grace, and love. By examining 2 Timothy alongside the teachings of Jesus and the other writings of Paul, we can better understand how to approach these themes with a spirit of humility and openness, rather than fear and division.

Titus, offering advice on church leadership and Christian living. However, when we examine the themes and writing of this letter, we can see why some aspects of it have raised concerns. It presents a view of Christian life and church organization that, while grounded in the need for order and sound doctrine, sometimes seems out of step with the inclusive and transformative message found throughout much of the New Testament. A closer look at the language and themes of Titus reveals some problematic elements that could be seen as contrary to the broader spirit of biblical scripture.

One issue lies in the letter's focus on the qualifications for church leadership. While it is important to have leaders who are faithful, mature, and capable of teaching, the specific qualifications listed in Titus seem to place a heavy emphasis on personal perfection. The letter calls for leaders to be "above reproach," "faithful to his wife," and "not arrogant." While these traits are valuable, the rigid standards set in Titus can make it seem as though only those who fit a certain mould are qualified to lead in the church. This narrow view of leadership risks excluding people who might have valuable insights and experiences but do not meet the strict requirements laid out in the letter. It also creates a form of elitism within the church that could lead to an environment where only those who adhere to a specific set of personal behaviours are seen as worthy of leadership. This contrasts with the message of Jesus, who often chose people from humble or unexpected backgrounds to be his closest followers, demonstrating that leadership in the Kingdom of god is not based on outward perfection but on inner transformation and the willingness to serve.

Another problematic theme in Titus is its treatment of women. While the letter encourages older women to teach the younger women how to live good Christian lives, it does so in a way that seems to reinforce traditional gender roles rather than challenging them. The letter advises women to focus on domestic duties, such as being "busy at home," "kind," and "submissive to their husbands." This language can be seen as limiting the roles of women within the church and society, suggesting that a woman's primary value lies in her ability to maintain a household and submit to male authority. Such an interpretation runs counter to the more egalitarian principles found in other parts of scripture, such as Galatians 3:28, where Paul writes that there is neither "Jew nor Greek, slave nor free, male nor female," implying that the gospel transcends social and gender boundaries. The emphasis on women's submission in Titus can be troubling because it reflects the social norms of the time, rather than the liberating message of the gospel that calls for equality and mutual respect in all relationships.

Titus also contains an admonition to "rebuke with all authority" and to "silence the rebellious people, especially those of the circumcision group." While it is certainly necessary to confront false teachings, the tone in Titus can come across as harsh and authoritarian. The call for leaders to assert their authority in such a forceful way might lead to a culture where dissent or disagreement is not allowed to flourish. This can be dangerous because it fosters an environment where only one interpretation of scripture is accepted, and questioning or differing viewpoints are seen as threats. The tendency to use "authority" as a means of silencing others can stifle healthy debate and the growth that comes from wrestling with difficult questions about faith. It's important to remember that the New Testament encourages believers to test teachings and hold fast to what is good, but Titus seems to present a model of leadership that emphasizes control over collaboration and humility.

The letter also makes statements about the nature of salvation and grace that are somewhat troubling when considered in light of the broader biblical message. For instance, Titus speaks about how "the grace of god has appeared that offers salvation to all people" and how Christians should "live self-controlled, upright, and godly lives." While the grace of god is central to the New Testament, the way it is framed in Titus could be seen as a call to moral perfectionism rather than a deeper understanding of grace as a transformative power. The letter seems to imply that living a godly life is a matter of simply following rules and being self-disciplined, which risks reducing the Christian faith to a set of external behaviours rather than a journey of inner renewal and transformation. This focus on outward conformity can create a sense of guilt or shame for those who struggle to meet these standards, rather than fostering an environment where believers are encouraged to grow in their relationship with god, regardless of their imperfections.

Additionally, Titus includes several warnings about the dangers of divisive people within the church. It tells the church to "warn a divisive person once, and then warn them a second time. After that, have nothing to do with them." While it's certainly important to protect the church from harmful teachings and division, this approach seems overly harsh. It suggests that people who cause division should be quickly cut off, rather than lovingly corrected or given the opportunity for reconciliation. This approach to dealing with conflict can create an atmosphere of exclusion, where individuals who might hold different views or who are struggling with their faith are simply dismissed. Instead of fostering a spirit of understanding and reconciliation, it can lead to a church culture where people are afraid to speak up or challenge the status quo for fear of being labelled as divisive.

Finally, there's the issue of Titus' approach to slaves. The letter encourages slaves to be "subject to their masters in everything" and to "please them not to talk back to them." While this was common in the first century world, this kind of language has been deeply problematic throughout history. When interpreted literally, it has been used to justify the oppression of enslaved people, with the implication that their submission is part of god's will. This is not the message we see in the broader scope of scripture, where the inherent dignity and equality of all people is emphasized. The teachings of Jesus and Paul, particularly in Galatians and Philemon, make it clear that slavery is a deeply flawed system and not something that aligns with the values of the Kingdom of god. The endorsement of the status quo of slavery in Titus seems out of place and at odds with the larger biblical call for justice and freedom.

When reading Titus in light of the whole of scripture, it's clear that the letter reflects some of the cultural attitudes and practices of its time. While it does contain valuable wisdom on church leadership and personal conduct, some of its themes can seem inconsistent with the broader gospel message of grace, love, and equality. The rigid qualifications for leadership, the restrictive view of women, the emphasis on authority over dialogue, and the treatment of slaves all point to a model of church and Christian life that is more about maintaining societal norms and control than about fostering genuine transformation and reconciliation in Christ. By carefully considering these issues, we can better understand how the teachings of Titus, like other parts of scripture, must be read in light of the overarching message of the gospel: a message of love, freedom, and equality for all people.

The book of 1 Peter, attributed to the Apostle Peter, is often seen as a letter meant to encourage Christians enduring persecution and suffering for their faith. However, when we look closer at the themes and language of 1 Peter, we find several aspects that might be troubling, especially when compared to the broader message of biblical mythology. These concerns revolve around its teachings on submission, suffering, and the role of women in the church, which seem to reflect the social and cultural norms of the time rather than a transformative message of freedom and equality.

One of the primary issues with 1 Peter is its repeated emphasis on submission, particularly in the context of relationships. The letter advises Christians to submit to governing authorities, to their masters, and even to their husbands in the case of women. While submission itself is not inherently problematic, the way it is framed in 1 Peter can be concerning. For example, the letter tells slaves to submit to their masters "with all respect" and encourages wives to submit to their husbands "so that, if any of them do not believe the word, they may be won over without words by the behaviour of their wives." This language, especially when read through a modern lens, can seem like an endorsement of submission for the sake of maintaining social order, rather than a call to challenge unjust systems or promote mutual respect and dignity in relationships. This approach can be harmful because it can perpetuate the idea that some individuals or groups should passively accept their circumstances, no matter how oppressive, in the name of spiritual submission. In contrast, the broader biblical message often calls for the overturning of systems of oppression and the recognition of the equality of all people before god.

Another problematic theme in 1 Peter is its treatment of suffering. While suffering for one's faith is a consistent theme in the New Testament, the way it is portrayed in 1 Peter may unintentionally glorify suffering in a way that overlooks the need for justice and relief from suffering. The letter encourages believers to "rejoice inasmuch as you participate in the sufferings of Christ" and views suffering as a way to identify with Jesus. While it is true that suffering can build character and deepen one's faith, the letter's focus on suffering could be seen as minimizing the need for social action to alleviate suffering and injustice. The call to endure suffering without complaint could be interpreted as a call for passivity, suggesting that Christians should simply accept suffering as a necessary part of the Christian life rather than actively working to challenge the conditions that cause suffering in the first place. This can be problematic because it risks promoting an attitude of passive resignation instead of a proactive, justice-driven faith that seeks to alleviate the suffering of others and work toward a more equitable world.

The role of women in 1 Peter is another area where the letter raises concerns. The letter advises women to have "the unfading beauty of a gentle and quiet spirit" and to submit to their husbands, even if they are unbelievers. While these instructions might have been culturally appropriate in the first century, they can be troubling when applied to modern contexts. The emphasis on a woman's beauty being tied to her submission and quietness can perpetuate harmful stereotypes about women's worth being found in their passivity and obedience rather than in their agency and ability to make their own choices. The idea that women should submit to their husbands to win them over to the faith can also be seen as reinforcing traditional gender roles and limiting women's roles in the church and society. This is at odds with the more radical biblical message of equality and mutual respect found elsewhere in the New Testament, such as in Galatians 3:28, which declares that there is neither "Jew nor Greek, slave nor free, male nor female" in Christ. The portrayal of women in 1 Peter as passive and submissive can be seen as a reflection of the cultural norms of the time rather than a call for the kind of freedom and empowerment that the gospel offers.

Another issue with 1 Peter is its treatment of the Christian community as a "royal priesthood" and a "holy nation." While these terms are meant to elevate the status of believers, they can also inadvertently reinforce an elitist mindset. The letter's language can make it seem as though Christians are set apart from the world in a way that makes them superior to others, which runs contrary to the message of humility and service that Jesus embodied. The call to be a "holy nation" can be interpreted as a form of spiritual nationalism that places believers in opposition to those outside the faith, rather than encouraging the church to be a community that reaches out to others with love and compassion. The idea of a "royal priesthood" might also be seen as reinforcing hierarchical structures within the church, where some individuals are seen as more spiritually important or closer to god than others. This can undermine the radical equality that the New Testament calls for, where all believers are seen as equal partners in the work of the Kingdom of god.

Finally, the letter's overall tone can sometimes seem dismissive of the broader social struggles of its time. While 1 Peter encourages believers to endure persecution with grace and to trust in god's ultimate justice, it doesn't provide much in the way of practical advice for addressing the systemic injustice and oppression that many of its readers would have been facing. The letter's focus on personal suffering and submission can overshadow the call for collective action to challenge the societal structures that cause harm. This can be seen as problematic because it risks turning the Christian faith into a passive acceptance of the status quo, rather than a transformative force that actively works to change the world for the better.

When we examine 1 Peter alongside the broader teachings of biblical mythology, we see that some of its themes seem to reflect the cultural and social norms of its time rather than the radical, transformative message of the gospel. The emphasis on submission, suffering, and gender roles can be troubling because it can reinforce systems of oppression and inequality rather than challenge them. While the letter certainly offers valuable wisdom for believers facing persecution, it is important to recognize that its message is shaped by the context in which it was written, and may not always align with the broader biblical call for justice, equality, and transformation. The challenge for modern readers is to interpret 1 Peter in a way that upholds the core message of the gospel while also being critical of the aspects that seem inconsistent with that message.

The book of 2 Peter is a curious one, and there are several aspects of it that have caused concern and raised eyebrows when it comes to aligning its message with the broader themes in biblical mythology. Whether it's the questionable authorship or some of its teachings, there are certain ideas in this letter that seem to contradict or complicate the more foundational messages found elsewhere in scripture. One of the primary problems with 2 Peter is its apparent endorsement of an authoritarian approach to leadership and its treatment of certain individuals and groups. This could be seen as contradictory to the broader biblical message of humility, servant leadership, and equality in Christ.

One of the biggest issues is how 2 Peter emphasizes the necessity of following leaders who claim to have special knowledge or authority. The letter speaks about false teachers and describes them in a way that implies that their teachings are dangerous because they lead people away from the "right way." In the context of a faith that promotes a personal relationship with god and direct access to the truth, this focus on hierarchical leadership feels off. When reading this letter, one might get the sense that it's less about individual discernment and more about submitting to a set of doctrines or church authorities. It's concerning because it seems to prioritize institutional authority over the personal and communal discernment that believers are encouraged to pursue throughout biblical mythology. The idea that there is a set of "right" teachers, who are in a position to tell others what to believe and how to live, doesn't align well with the more egalitarian aspects of biblical teachings, which speak to the responsibility of each individual believer to grow in knowledge and truth.

Another issue with 2 Peter is its treatment of the second coming of Christ. The letter talks about the return of Christ and the destruction of the world, and it uses imagery that can be unsettling or difficult to reconcile with the hope and peace that are found elsewhere in scripture. The text speaks about a world being destroyed by fire and the righteous being vindicated in this apocalyptic event. The problem here is that this imagery often leads to an idea of judgment that feels harsh and unyielding. While it's true that biblical mythology speaks about the return of Christ bringing about justice, the emphasis in 2 Peter on a final, fiery judgment can seem extreme. It runs the risk of reducing the narrative of salvation to an impending catastrophe for those who don't measure up, rather than focusing on the transformative love and grace that are central to the gospel. It's easy for readers to focus on the wrath and destruction, forgetting the emphasis elsewhere in biblical mythology on god's desire to save and restore all people.

There's also a certain tension in 2 Peter with regard to the timing of Christ's return. The letter begins with a bit of a reprimand for those who have been waiting too long, with people questioning why Christ hasn't come back yet. The writer tries to answer this by saying that time is different for god, that a thousand years are like a day to him, and that god is being patient. On one hand, this is comforting, as it suggests that god's delays are for our benefit, but on the other hand, this presents a theological problem. The idea of god "waiting" for something, in a sense, challenges the understanding of god's perfect plan unfolding according to his will. It suggests that there is something lacking in god's immediate fulfillment of his promises. This idea of divine delay creates some tension in the broader biblical narrative, where god's timing is often presented as perfect and unchanging. The apparent need for god to wait for the right time to return introduces a human understanding of time that feels contradictory to the timeless nature of the divine.

The way 2 Peter treats the Old Testament scriptures is also worth noting. The letter emphasizes the reliability of the prophetic word, particularly pointing to the experiences of those who witnessed Christ's transfiguration. It asserts that the prophetic word is more reliable than personal experiences, which seems to elevate the written scriptures as the ultimate source of authority. While this emphasis on the scriptures is certainly important, the way it is framed in 2 Peter can come across as undermining the value of personal experience and the active, relational experience of god that many believers might encounter in their day-to-day lives. The letter seems to suggest that truth is found primarily in the written word and not in the lived experience of faith, which can be problematic. Throughout biblical mythology, we find numerous examples where god interacts with people in deeply personal and experiential ways. To suggest that scripture alone is the only valid source of truth can feel limiting, especially when considering the fullness of the biblical message about how god reveals himself to humanity in various ways.

Another key issue in 2 Peter is its treatment of the idea of grace. The letter warns against those who "twist" the scriptures to justify immorality or self-serving behaviour. It speaks harshly against such people, and while this may seem like a call to righteous living, there's an underlying implication that grace is conditional. The letter suggests that there is a point at which people who stray from the truth become too far gone to be saved. This contradicts the more inclusive message of grace found elsewhere in biblical mythology, where god's grace is seen as available to all who repent and turn to him. While 2 Peter certainly warns against false teaching and encourages believers to be diligent in their faith, it also seems to introduce a kind of "cut-off" point, after which grace no longer applies. This is a problem because it undercuts the transformative power of grace, which is central to the Christian message. If grace is truly as expansive as biblical mythology suggests, then it should be seen as always available, not something that can be forfeited through error or disobedience.

Looking at 2 Peter, it's clear that some of its themes and teachings seem at odds with the more overarching messages of biblical mythology. The letter's emphasis on submission to authority, its portrayal of god's delay in returning, its harsh apocalyptic imagery, and its ideas about the limits of grace and the role of scripture all introduce ideas that feel problematic when set alongside the broader narrative of god's love, justice, and mercy. While 2 Peter certainly has some valuable points to make about the dangers of false teaching and the importance of living faithfully, it also brings up some theological concerns that make it harder to reconcile with the broader biblical message of inclusion, transformation, and love. This doesn't necessarily mean that 2 Peter should be dismissed, but it does invite a deeper reflection on how we interpret its messages and how they fit into the full scope of biblical truth.

Revelation

The book of Revelation has long been a source of fascination and controversy. Many people approach it with a sense of mystery, trying to decode its cryptic visions and symbols. The imagery in Revelation is vivid and often disturbing, filled with strange beasts, apocalyptic destruction, and divine judgments. But when we take a closer look, it's clear that some of the themes in Revelation raise significant questions about how they fit into the larger biblical narrative, especially when it comes to the nature of god and the message of the gospel.

One of the biggest issues with Revelation is its depiction of divine wrath. The book presents a vivid picture of god unleashing destruction upon the earth, with natural disasters, wars, and plagues wreaking havoc on humanity. The most troubling aspect of this is the portrayal of god as actively orchestrating these terrifying events, which seems at odds with the image of a loving and merciful god that we find throughout the rest of biblical mythology. God's actions in Revelation, as described, often come across as wrathful and vengeful, and this raises the question of how this fits into the broader story of salvation that is at the heart of the gospel. Revelation depicts a god who punishes the wicked with finality, and this can seem harsh compared to the portrayal of god as long-suffering and full of grace in other parts of biblical mythology. The focus on judgment in Revelation, while it may reflect the reality of divine justice, can overshadow the broader message of mercy, forgiveness, and redemption that is central to the Christian faith.

The apocalyptic language in Revelation also has a tendency to emphasize fear and hopelessness. While the book is filled with imagery of ultimate triumph for the faithful, it often feels as if the narrative is one of inevitable destruction. The focus on the end of the world, the battle between good and evil, and the final judgment can create a sense of urgency and fear, as if salvation is something that can only be attained by surviving the terrifying cataclysms that precede it. This could lead believers to focus more on the horrors of the future than on the present reality of living out their faith. The idea of a final judgment, in which only a select few are saved, creates a fear-based theology that can be harmful to the spiritual life of individuals who may feel uncertain about their place in god's plan. It runs the risk of turning faith into something that is primarily concerned with avoiding catastrophe rather than experiencing the fullness of life in Christ.

Another problematic aspect of Revelation is its treatment of the concept of exclusivity. The book often emphasizes that only a certain group of people will be saved, and those who do not belong to that group will face eternal damnation. The imagery of the "mark of the beast" and the "lake of fire" is meant to distinguish the faithful from the unfaithful, but it can also perpetuate a sense of division and exclusion. This is problematic because it contradicts the more inclusive message of the gospel, where Jesus' invitation to salvation is extended to all people, regardless of their background or past behaviour. The idea that only a select few will be saved runs the risk of reinforcing the belief that salvation is about belonging to the right group rather than about personal transformation, repentance, and grace. It also leads to the potential for division and judgment within the Christian community, where some may view themselves as more deserving of salvation than others.

There's also the issue of Revelation's historical context. Many scholars believe that the book was written during a time of intense persecution of early Christians, possibly during the reign of the Roman Emperor Domitian. In this context, the book's vivid imagery can be seen as a form of protest against the oppressive regime, offering hope to believers by assuring them that justice would ultimately prevail. However, this context doesn't always translate well to modern readers, who may approach the text with a different set of assumptions about power, authority, and persecution. When read without an understanding of the historical situation, the imagery in Revelation can seem unnecessarily violent or catastrophic, leading to misunderstandings about its purpose. The book's symbolism is rooted in the historical and political realities of the time, but if that context is ignored, it can be misinterpreted as a literal prophecy about the future rather than a timely message of hope for people under oppression.

Another theme in Revelation that has sparked debate is its treatment of the church and its role in the end times. The letters to the seven churches in Asia Minor offer a stern warning about the dangers of complacency, false teaching, and spiritual apathy. While these warnings are important, they also contribute to the overall tone of judgment and condemnation that pervades the book. It's easy to read these messages and focus on the harsh rebukes rather than the call to repentance and transformation. The letter to the Laodiceans, in particular, has often been interpreted as a condemnation of lukewarm faith, but this can create an unhealthy sense of guilt and shame. Instead of emphasizing personal growth and transformation, it can make people feel as though they are constantly falling short, never able to live up to the standards set in Revelation.

The figure of the Antichrist, also prominent in Revelation, is another aspect that has sparked considerable concern. The image of a powerful, evil figure who deceives the world and leads people away from god can be alarming, and the emphasis on identifying this figure can sometimes lead to fear and obsession with external threats. The idea that an ultimate enemy of Christ will arise in the future can shift the focus away from the ongoing battle between good and evil that plays out in our lives daily. Instead of focusing on personal spiritual growth and the fight against sin, Revelation's apocalyptic vision can encourage believers to look for an external, future figure to personify evil. This can detract from the real work of resisting temptation, living in integrity, and working for justice and peace in the present.

Revelation has long been a book that challenges us, and many of its themes continue to create tension within the Christian community. The book's focus on judgment, exclusivity, and apocalyptic destruction stands in stark contrast to the messages of grace, mercy, and inclusion found elsewhere in biblical mythology. While Revelation may be meant to encourage perseverance in the face of suffering, it also carries themes that can easily be misused to create fear, division, and exclusion. When reading Revelation, we need to be careful to interpret it in light of the broader biblical story, remembering that god's ultimate purpose is not destruction but redemption. Finally, we must seriously consider the possibility that such a work that stands alone in stark contrast to the majority of biblical mythology should not be part of biblical mythology.

Eidotheosophy is not about dismantling or replacing religion. It's a philosophy that seeks to refine our understanding of spiritual truth by separating what is divine from what is human. This isn't an exercise in rejection or deconstruction but an effort to thoughtfully sift through the layers of religious texts and traditions to uncover wisdom that might genuinely come from a higher source. This approach doesn't erase the foundation of any belief system but instead offers tools to engage with it in a way that emphasizes logic, reason, and a commitment to the well-being of humanity.

What makes eidotheosophy unique is its adaptability. It's not tethered exclusively to biblical mythology, even though that's where I've chosen to apply it in my work. The methodology, using research, historical context, and rational thinking to assess religious teachings, can be applied to any spiritual framework. Whether someone is engaging with the Quran, the Vedas, the Tripitaka, or any other sacred text, the principles of eidotheosophy remain the same. The goal is to carefully examine what has been taught and distinguish between divine intent and human interference. This approach respects the sacred while recognizing that humans have a tendency to infuse their own agendas into religion, often to the detriment of others.

The flexibility of eidotheosophy opens the door to shared dialogue between belief systems. By its nature, it's not bound to one interpretation or tradition but instead invites a deeper exploration of truth across all spiritual paths. If someone were to adapt eidotheosophy to their own religion, the core principles wouldn't change. The focus would still be on understanding divine wisdom through reason and ensuring that human interpretations don't overshadow ethical and spiritual truths. What would differ, though, is the starting point. The central narrative, figures, and teachings of a religion would shape how its followers embark on their spiritual journeys.

Even with these differences in focus, the shared framework of eidotheosophy creates space for common ground. The questions we ask and the tools we use to seek answers are fundamentally similar, regardless of religious background. What does this text teach about humanity's purpose? How do these teachings align with what we know about the world and human nature? Are there practices or beliefs that harm others or limit progress? When religions adopt this kind of introspection, the barriers between them begin to dissolve. The focus shifts from competition over who holds the "absolute truth" to a shared pursuit of understanding and meaning.

Adopting eidotheosophy across different religions could foster a spirit of collaboration. When religions no longer cling to dogmas as unassailable truths but instead view them as starting points for deeper inquiry, it becomes easier to share ideas and learn from one another. Each tradition brings its own wisdom and perspective, and through dialogue, these can enrich one another. By focusing on ethical outcomes and the shared human experience, religions can evolve into forces that work together to promote peace, justice, and understanding rather than conflict and division.

What I find most compelling about this possibility is that it allows for unity without demanding uniformity. Eidotheosophy doesn't insist that everyone interpret divine wisdom the same way. It respects the diversity of thought and experience that shapes each person's journey. What it does demand is that we approach our beliefs critically and with humility, recognizing that no single interpretation holds all the answers. This mindset encourages both personal growth and mutual respect, which are essential for navigating a world where so many different belief systems coexist.

Eidotheosophy also challenges the notion that religions must be insular. Often, religious communities are wary of outside influence, fearing that engagement with other ideologies will dilute their faith or undermine their authority. But when you strip away the fear and look at the shared values and goals across religions, it becomes clear that collaboration doesn't threaten faith; it strengthens it. When we open ourselves to the idea that truth can be found in many places and that divine wisdom isn't confined to one text or tradition, we create an environment where faith becomes more resilient, not less.

The beauty of eidotheosophy is that it doesn't ask anyone to abandon their religious identity. Instead, it invites believers to dig deeper, to question, and to grow. It's a philosophy that honours the sacred while refusing to ignore the flaws in how humans have interpreted the divine. For those willing to embrace this process, the result is not only a richer understanding of their own faith but also a greater capacity to connect with others. At its heart, eidotheosophy is about fostering a spirituality that is thoughtful, inclusive, and grounded in both reason and compassion.

Conceiving Eidotheosophy

Exploring the interplay between faith and reason has been a deeply personal journey for me. Like many, I had the impression that faith required unquestioning belief and that reason operated in an entirely separate space. The two seemed at odds, with one demanding trust in the unseen and the other insisting on evidence and logic. This tension felt unnecessary, even counterproductive, so I set out to reconcile these two forces in a way that honoured both the spiritual depth of faith and the intellectual rigour of reason. This exploration gave rise to eidotheosophy, a framework designed to help believers evaluate divine wisdom with tools grounded in sound logic, reason, and objective facts.

Eidotheosophy is not about discarding faith in favour of science or reducing spirituality to academic formulas. Instead, it's about creating a space where both can coexist and enrich one another. Faith, at its best, inspires and guides us, offering meaning and purpose. Reason, meanwhile, helps us test ideas, challenge assumptions, and build frameworks for understanding the world. Together, they can provide a more balanced approach to exploring questions of divine wisdom, ensuring that what we believe is not only spiritually meaningful but also intellectually sound.

Academic research, philosophy, and social sciences play a key role in this paradigm. These disciplines give us tools to examine the cultural, historical, and psychological contexts that shape our understanding of spiritual concepts. For example, by studying the historical development of biblical mythology, we can see how divine wisdom has been interpreted, reinterpreted, and sometimes distorted over time. This doesn't diminish the value of biblical mythology; if anything, it highlights its resilience and adaptability. By approaching these texts with an open but critical mind, we can separate enduring truths from human biases and cultural artifacts.

Philosophy contributes a wealth of thought about ethics, morality, and the nature of existence. These ideas complement spiritual teachings by providing a logical structure for understanding concepts like justice, love, and purpose. Social sciences, on the other hand, allow us to study how faith operates in human communities, how beliefs are formed and transmitted, and how they influence behaviour and decision-making. These insights are crucial for understanding not just what we believe but why we believe it and how those beliefs impact the world.

This approach does require a shift in how we think about faith. It asks believers to embrace complexity, uncertainty, and the possibility that some cherished ideas might not hold up under scrutiny. But it also offers something valuable in return; a faith that is not only deeply personal but also robust enough to withstand challenges and questions. It encourages believers to see doubt not as a threat but as an invitation to explore more deeply. In doing so, it transforms faith from something static into something dynamic and evolving.

Eidotheosophy isn't meant to replace traditional approaches to faith but to complement them. For those who find comfort in traditional interpretations, this framework can provide additional depth and perspective. For those who struggle with reconciling faith and reason, it offers a pathway to engage with spiritual concepts without abandoning intellectual integrity. It doesn't demand that we have all the answers; it simply invites us to ask better questions and to approach those questions with both humility and curiosity.

Ultimately, eidotheosophy serves as a bridge between faith and reason, providing a more intellectually satisfying framework for understanding divine wisdom. It allows us to honour the spiritual truths that have shaped humanity for centuries while also engaging with the tools of modern thought and inquiry. In doing so, it offers a way to make faith not just a personal journey but a shared exploration of what it means to seek wisdom, to live well, and to connect with the divine.

Subjective Experience And Objective Communication

Subjective experience is one of the most profound aspects of human existence. Each of us navigates life through a lens shaped by personal encounters, emotions, and perceptions. These experiences are deeply intimate, often difficult to articulate fully, and uniquely tied to who we are. The richness of subjectivity, however, presents a challenge when we try to communicate it to others. Language, while powerful, has inherent limitations. It is structured and shared, but the most profound parts of our inner lives often transcend what words can capture. The tension between what we feel and what we can say is a fascinating part of human expression.

When discussing subjective experiences, especially in the context of spiritual encounters, this challenge becomes even more pronounced. How do we describe something so deeply personal that it feels beyond the confines of language? Biblical mythology grapples with this difficulty by using stories, parables, and poetry to communicate ideas that might otherwise defy direct description. These creative forms allow room for interpretation, offering readers a way to connect with the underlying truths through their own experiences. However, even these inspired narratives cannot fully convey the essence of the divine encounters they attempt to describe.

Humans, recognizing the limits of words, have devised creative ways to express their inner worlds objectively. Music, for instance, becomes a language of its own, translating emotion into melody and rhythm. A piece of music can convey joy, sorrow, or awe in ways that resonate universally, even without lyrics. Similarly, visual art allows people to capture feelings and perspectives that words might flatten or obscure. A painting or sculpture communicates in textures and colours, opening a space for viewers to connect with the artist's experience on their own terms.

In academic research and philosophy, there is a growing recognition of the need to address subjective experience with sensitivity and precision. Scholars study how humans construct meaning from their experiences and explore frameworks to bridge the gap between subjective and objective realities. In psychology, for example, narrative therapy invites individuals to tell their stories as a way of understanding their personal truths and creating a bridge to shared understanding. This practice acknowledges that while each story is deeply personal, the act of telling it creates a connection with others.

Biblical mythology itself serves as a testament to humanity's enduring effort to make subjective experiences accessible and meaningful to others. The metaphors, imagery, and symbolic language in these texts attempt to communicate encounters with the divine, moral insights, and existential questions. While these accounts are often rooted in the subjective experiences of their authors, they provide a framework for readers to engage with similar ideas in their own lives. The stories may not always be literal, but their power lies in their ability to evoke shared emotions and reflections.

Even in everyday communication, we find ways to bridge the gap between subjective and objective worlds. We use analogies, comparisons, and shared cultural references to explain feelings and experiences. Phrases like "it felt like my heart was on fire" may not be literal, but they offer a glimpse into an internal experience in a way others can understand. Humour, too, often arises from shared experiences that resonate universally, connecting individuals through the recognition of a common truth.

The interplay between subjective experience and objective communication is both a challenge and an opportunity. While the limitations of language can feel frustrating, they also drive creativity and innovation. Whether through art, storytelling, or conversation, we continually strive to make our inner lives comprehensible to others. This process is not just about sharing information; it is about building connection, understanding, and empathy. In the context of faith and philosophy, this becomes even more vital, as it allows individuals to explore complex and deeply personal questions together, finding common ground in the shared human pursuit of meaning.

Eidotheosophy And Logical Inquiry

Eidotheosophy sits at the crossroads of belief and rationality. At its heart, it seeks to reconcile faith with the principles of logical inquiry, offering a spiritual framework that does not abandon reason but embraces it as an essential tool for understanding divine wisdom. In this way, eidotheosophy draws from the rich traditions of philosophical thought, threading its narrative through centuries of intellectual exploration. It does not see belief and logic as opposing forces but as complementary aspects of the human quest for meaning and truth.

The relationship between eidotheosophy and logical reasoning begins with a shared commitment to questioning assumptions. Logical inquiry thrives on skepticism, challenging claims and demanding evidence. Eidotheosophy mirrors this process by encouraging believers to critically examine their understanding of divine wisdom. It invites a closer look at the origins of religious teachings, the motivations behind human interpretations, and the societal implications of theological doctrines. This approach acknowledges that faith, to be truly meaningful, must withstand the scrutiny of reason.

Eidotheosophy owes much of its intellectual foundation to the traditions of philosophical reasoning. Ancient thinkers like Socrates and Aristotle emphasized the importance of questioning and dialogue in the pursuit of truth. Socratic dialogue, with its emphasis on asking probing questions to uncover underlying beliefs, resonates deeply with the spirit of eidotheosophy. Similarly, Aristotle's insistence on the use of logic to build knowledge provides a framework for understanding how spiritual ideas can be analyzed and evaluated.

What sets eidotheosophy apart is its willingness to apply logical reasoning directly to spiritual questions. It does not shy away from the complexities of metaphysical concepts or the challenges of interpreting divine wisdom. Instead, it embraces these difficulties as opportunities for growth. By encouraging believers to explore their faith through a lens of reason, eidotheosophy transforms spiritual exploration into an active, dynamic process. This stands in contrast to more dogmatic approaches, which often discourage questioning in favour of unquestioning acceptance.

Eidotheosophy also draws from the Enlightenment tradition, which championed the power of reason to advance knowledge and improve society. Thinkers like John Locke and Immanuel Kant emphasized the role of rational thought in understanding the world and navigating moral questions. Eidotheosophy aligns with this legacy by asserting that faith need not be blind to reason. Instead, it can engage with reason to form a more coherent and compassionate understanding of divine wisdom.

In practice, eidotheosophy employs logical tools to parse the layers of biblical mythology and distinguish between human interpretations and divine insights. It recognizes that religious texts often carry the imprint of the cultures and societies that produced them. By analyzing these texts through historical and academic lenses, eidotheosophy seeks to uncover universal principles that transcend their time-bound origins. This process relies on logical reasoning to separate enduring wisdom from the biases and limitations of human authorship.

At its core, eidotheosophy affirms the value of reasoned exploration as a path to deeper understanding. It acknowledges that faith, like any other aspect of human experience, can be enriched by engaging with the principles of logical inquiry. This does not mean reducing spiritual beliefs to a series of proofs or equations. Rather, it means approaching faith with the same intellectual rigour we apply to other areas of life, fostering a more authentic and thoughtful relationship with divine wisdom.

Eidotheosophy stands as an intellectual heir to the great traditions of philosophical thought. It builds on the foundations laid by generations of thinkers who sought to understand the world and our place in it. By weaving its narrative through the threads of logical inquiry, eidotheosophy bridges the gap between belief and reason, offering a way to navigate the complexities of faith with clarity and purpose. In doing so, it creates a space where spiritual exploration and intellectual growth can coexist, each enriching the other in the shared pursuit of truth.

Descartes's "Cogito, Ergo Sum"

At the centre of Descartes's philosophy is the principle expressed as "I think, therefore I am." This phrase is deceptively simple but carries profound implications for how we understand knowledge, existence, and self-awareness. When Descartes articulated this idea in his "Meditations on First Philosophy," he was grappling with the problem of doubt. By systematically questioning everything he believed to be true, Descartes sought to strip away all uncertainty and find a foundation upon which he could build reliable knowledge. This principle became that foundation, the one unshakable truth he could not doubt.

What makes this principle so compelling is its immediacy. Descartes realized that even if he doubted everything, including his senses, his memories, and even the existence of an external world, he could not doubt the act of doubting itself. Doubt, after all, is a form of thinking, and thinking presupposes a thinker. This insight gave Descartes a point of absolute certainty: the existence of the self as a thinking entity. This principle is not just a statement about existence; it is a profound declaration of the self's undeniable reality, anchored in the act of thought.

This principle 's significance extends beyond its role as a philosophical foundation. It redefined the way we think about the self and its relationship to knowledge. Before Descartes, much of philosophical thought was grounded in external authorities, such as religious texts, traditions, or communal beliefs. By centring the act of thinking as the basis of certainty, Descartes shifted the focus inward. Knowledge became something rooted in the individual's capacity for reason rather than something imposed from without. This was a revolutionary idea, laying the groundwork for modern philosophy's emphasis on autonomy and critical thinking.

This principle also underscores a fundamental tension between subjective experience and objective knowledge. While Descartes found certainty in the act of thinking, this certainty is deeply personal. It is something only the individual can directly experience. For someone else, the existence of the thinking self is not self-evident; it must be inferred. This raises questions about the nature of knowledge and how we can share subjective truths in ways that resonate universally. Descartes's insight reminds us that even our most certain truths are intimately tied to our own perspectives, a theme that resonates with many modern discussions in epistemology.

In historical context, this principle was a response to the uncertainties of Descartes's time. The seventeenth century was an era of intellectual upheaval, with traditional sources of authority increasingly questioned by scientific discoveries and new philosophical ideas. Descartes sought to provide a stable foundation in a world that seemed increasingly unstable. By grounding certainty in the thinking self, he offered a way to navigate these uncertainties without abandoning the quest for truth. This principle became not just a philosophical principle but a lifeline for those seeking clarity in a rapidly changing world.

What makes this principle particularly relevant today is its emphasis on the interplay between doubt and certainty. In an age where information is abundant and often conflicting, the ability to question and critically examine our beliefs is more important than ever. Descartes's method of radical doubt reminds us that questioning is not a sign of weakness but a pathway to deeper understanding. At the same time, this principle reminds us that some truths, like that of our own existence, can withstand even the most rigorous scrutiny.

This principle has not been without its critics. Some argue that it assumes too much, that the leap from "thinking exists" to "a thinker exists" is not as airtight as Descartes claimed. Others suggest that it overly isolates the self, ignoring the ways in which our thoughts are shaped by relationships, culture, and the broader world. These critiques highlight this principle's limitations but also its enduring relevance. Even as we challenge its assumptions, we engage with its core insight: that the act of thinking reveals something profound about the nature of existence.

Descartes's principle is more than a philosophical statement; it is an invitation to reflect on what it means to know and to be. By grounding certainty in the thinking self, Descartes gave us a tool for navigating the uncertainties of life with clarity and purpose. Whether we embrace or critique his ideas, this principle continues to shape the way we think about ourselves and our place in the world.

The Other In Phenomenology

Phenomenology offers an intriguing lens for exploring the interplay between consciousness, perception, and the divine, particularly when it intersects with the ideas central to eidotheosophy. At its core, phenomenology concerns itself with how individuals experience and interpret the world, emphasizing the structures of consciousness that shape our engagement with reality. It is not merely a method of inquiry; it is a way of understanding how we relate to ourselves, others, and the broader context of existence. In theological exploration, phenomenology takes on a unique significance, providing tools to examine the relationship between humanity and the divine.

In the human experience, much of what defines identity emerges through a contrast with the perceived Other. This is one of phenomenology's most compelling contributions. It highlights how the boundaries of self-awareness are often drawn in opposition to what we perceive as external to us. The concept of alterity, the recognition of difference, is central here. By encountering something outside ourselves, whether another person or an idea, we gain clarity about who we are. This process is not inherently antagonistic; it is simply the mechanism by which individuality asserts itself. We come to know ourselves through relationships, comparisons, and distinctions.

When applied to theology, this idea becomes even more profound. The divine, particularly as understood in biblical mythology, often represents the ultimate Other. It is something so wholly different from the human that it defies easy comprehension, yet it is also intimately connected to us. In eidotheosophy, this dynamic is especially relevant when we consider the holy spirit. Perception of the holy spirit is inherently subjective, mediated through personal experiences and shaped by the cultural and theological frameworks in which one is immersed. However, it is also collective, creating a shared sense of divine presence that transcends individual understanding.

The holy spirit, within this framework, becomes both a marker of divine alterity and a bridge to divine intimacy. It embodies the paradox of being wholly Other and yet profoundly present. Phenomenologically, this reflects a unique kind of consciousness; one that perceives not just the self in relation to other humans, but the self in relation to something far greater. The holy spirit's perceived presence challenges and reshapes the boundaries of identity, inviting individuals to see themselves not just as isolated beings but as part of a larger, interconnected spiritual reality.

Eidotheosophy, in its effort to reconcile faith and reason, engages with these ideas by encouraging believers to approach the divine through both personal experience and logical inquiry. Phenomenology provides a way to understand how individuals might perceive the holy spirit as an influence that transcends the purely intellectual. It is not simply about believing in the holy spirit as a concept; it is about encountering it as a lived reality. This encounter, though deeply personal, resonates with universal themes of connection, guidance, and transformation.

The act of perceiving the holy spirit, like all phenomenological experiences, is shaped by context. Historical and cultural factors play a significant role in how people understand and articulate their encounters with the divine. Biblical mythology provides a wealth of narratives that illustrate this. The stories of prophets, disciples, and other figures often centre on moments of divine encounter, such times when the holy spirit acts as both a disruptor of ordinary life and a catalyst for extraordinary change. These narratives serve as archetypes for how people today might understand their own experiences with the divine.

Eidotheosophy emphasizes the importance of critically examining these perceptions. It does not seek to diminish their spiritual significance, but rather to understand them more fully. By applying the principles of phenomenology, believers can explore how their experiences of the holy spirit are influenced by their consciousness, their context, and their community. This approach does not undermine faith; it deepens it, offering a richer, more nuanced understanding of what it means to perceive and interact with the divine.

The relationship between phenomenology, theology, and eidotheosophy is ultimately one of exploration. It is about navigating the complex terrain of human consciousness to find meaning in the divine. In this journey, the holy spirit emerges as a central figure; a manifestation of the divine that challenges, transforms, and inspires. Through the lens of phenomenology, we can begin to appreciate the depth of this relationship and the ways it shapes both individual identity and collective understanding.

Schrödinger's Cat And God's Quantum Superposition

The pursuit of understanding the divine within eidotheosophy often requires creative approaches to reconcile spiritual concepts with rational thought. One of the more intriguing intersections in this exploration lies between the metaphysical aspects of religious perception and the principles of quantum mechanics. Schrödinger's Cat, a famous thought experiment, provides a fascinating metaphor for understanding how belief and nonbelief in god coexist within the same reality, with the holy spirit playing a pivotal role as the perceived intermediary between humanity and the divine.

In Schrödinger's thought experiment, a cat placed inside a sealed box with a mechanism that has a 50-50 chance of killing it exists in a state of quantum superposition. Until the box is opened and observed, the cat is simultaneously alive and dead. This paradox challenges our classical understanding of reality and forces us to consider how observation itself shapes what we perceive to be true. While this experiment is primarily a tool for illustrating quantum principles, it serves as a compelling analogy for the metaphysical complexities of divine perception.

From the standpoint of believers, god's presence is as real and tangible as the beating of their own hearts. The holy spirit, within this framework, acts as the bridge between the seen and the unseen, providing a sense of connection to the divine that is deeply felt and transformative. This presence is not merely theoretical for believers; it is experiential. For them, the evidence of god's existence is woven into their daily lives, manifested in moments of inspiration, comfort, and guidance attributed to the holy spirit's influence.

On the other hand, nonbelievers encounter the same world with a vastly different perception. For them, the absence of tangible evidence for god leads to the equally valid proposition that god does not exist. They might interpret what believers call the holy spirit as psychological phenomena, cultural constructs, or neurological responses. Their observation of reality does not include the divine, and thus, in their perspective, the box has been opened to reveal a world without god.

This duality, where god both exists and does not exist depending on the observer, is where Schrödinger's Cat becomes a useful metaphor. In a sense, god and the holy spirit exist in a kind of metaphysical superposition. Their existence or absence is determined not by some objective reality but by the framework of belief through which they are perceived. For believers, opening the box reveals a living, active divine presence. For nonbelievers, the box is opened to reveal its absence. Both experiences are internally consistent and rational within their respective worldviews.

This analogy aligns well with the principles of eidotheosophy, which encourages a balanced exploration of faith and reason. It acknowledges that belief in god, facilitated by the holy spirit, is deeply subjective and personal, shaped by cultural, emotional, and intellectual factors. At the same time, it respects the rational standpoint of nonbelief, which is grounded in observable evidence, or the lack thereof. Eidotheosophy does not seek to prove or disprove god's existence; instead, it embraces the idea that such questions may ultimately depend on the observer's perspective.

The metaphor also emphasizes the role of the holy spirit as a dynamic and subjective experience. For believers, the holy spirit is not an abstract concept but an active presence that provides meaning and guidance. For nonbelievers, the holy spirit is nothing more than a construct; it's a product of human imagination or collective psychology. This dual perception underscores the complexity of discussing divine phenomena in a way that respects both faith and reason.

By framing the question of god's existence in terms of quantum superposition, eidotheosophy offers a way to understand how belief systems can coexist without contradiction. It allows for the possibility that the divine is not a binary proposition of existence or nonexistence but something far more nuanced, shaped by individual experience and perception. This perspective does not diminish the importance of belief; rather, it enriches it by highlighting the profound ways in which humans engage with the unknown. Whether one perceives god as present or absent, the exploration of such questions opens pathways to deeper understanding, both of oneself and of the broader human experience.

The Influence Of The Holy Spirit

When diving into the Christian faith through the lens of eidotheosophy, one of the fundamental questions that arises is whether god intervenes directly in human affairs or if god's influence is mediated through the holy spirit. This question isn't just a matter of theological curiosity but speaks to deeper concerns about the nature of divine action, human agency, and the problem of evil. If god acts directly in the world, it raises immediate questions about free will; whether god's direct involvement negates human agency and choice. It also brings up difficult issues, such as why god allows suffering and why evil seems to persist despite the promise of a loving, omnipotent creator. On the other hand, if god's influence operates primarily through the holy spirit, then we are left with the task of understanding how this indirect influence works. How do we discern the divine will in the midst of our everyday lives? And what role do we play in co-creating our reality with god's guidance through the holy spirit?

In the framework of eidotheosophy, god is understood to influence human beings primarily through the holy spirit, which acts as a subtle guide and communicator between the divine and the individual. This idea introduces a nuanced perspective on divine interaction. The holy spirit doesn't force decisions or dictate every action but instead acts as an influence that can inspire, nudge, or gently correct. The holy spirit is not a puppet master but rather a loving presence that guides believers toward a deeper understanding of divine wisdom. This concept allows for a dynamic relationship between humans and the divine; one where the individual still has agency and can make choices, but those choices are informed by a higher wisdom that can be felt and experienced through the holy spirit.

A key feature of this model is that it does not eliminate human responsibility or agency. Instead of god intervening directly in the world, shaping every moment and directing every outcome, the holy spirit works within individuals, planting seeds of understanding, prompting reflections, and offering guidance. This influence, though subtle, is powerful and can lead to profound changes in the way people think, act, and interact with the world. The holy spirit can be perceived as an ongoing presence in a person's life, one that challenges them to live according to divine wisdom, love, and justice, but without coercion.

This approach to divine influence, when considered through the lens of eidotheosophy, raises some interesting questions about how we understand the mechanics of the holy spirit's impact. If god operates in this indirect way, how do we know when the influence we feel is truly divine and not just a product of our own imagination, or thoughts, or desires? This is where the idea of discernment becomes critical. Discernment, in this context, is the ability to distinguish between divine influence and personal impulse. It requires a deep attentiveness to the subtle workings of the spirit in one's life; an awareness that comes with practice, reflection, and spiritual growth. Discernment is not always easy, and the line between divine prompting and personal will can be difficult to draw. Yet, for those who seek it, the holy spirit's guidance can become clearer over time, as it aligns with the teachings of love, justice, and compassion that are foundational in the biblical narrative.

The nature of the holy spirit's influence also brings up the question of how this affects the balance between human agency and spiritual influence. If god acts indirectly through the holy spirit, there is still room for humans to make their own decisions and act in the world. But those actions are shaped by the spirit's guidance, which means that individuals are not acting purely out of self-interest or worldly desires. Instead, they are acting in alignment with a higher purpose, one that aims to bring about a better world for all people. This doesn't mean that humans become passive or merely follow orders from some divine master. Rather, it means that they are empowered by the spirit to make choices that reflect divine wisdom and love, even when those choices are difficult or unpopular.

This model of divine influence also aligns with the role of Jesus as the divine teacher in Christian mythology. Jesus is presented in the Gospels as the ultimate example of living according to divine wisdom and love. He teaches by example, showing how to live with compassion, forgiveness, and justice, even in the face of adversity. In this sense, the holy spirit's influence can be seen as the ongoing presence of Jesus' teachings in the world; an invisible but powerful force that continues to inspire and guide believers to live in a way that reflects the values he embodied. Jesus, as the divine teacher, set a path for others to follow, and the holy spirit helps to guide those who seek to walk that path today.

The idea of divine influence through the holy spirit, as explored in eidotheosophy, allows for a richer understanding of the relationship between god, human agency, and suffering. It provides a way to understand how god might work in the world without directly intervening in every situation. Instead, the divine works within the hearts and minds of individuals, shaping their actions and helping them to align with higher principles of love and justice. This doesn't eliminate the challenges and suffering that people face, but it offers a way to navigate those challenges in a way that reflects divine wisdom. Ultimately, this model of divine influence respects both human agency and the possibility of spiritual guidance, creating a balanced and dynamic relationship between the believer and the divine.

www.ingramcontent.com/pod-product-compliance
Lightning Source LLC
Chambersburg PA
CBHW071500140726
47997CB00005B/1799